Beyond the Mist

Beyond the Mist

The Story of
Donald and Dorothy Fairley

David C. Thompson, MD

Christian Publications, Inc.
Camp Hill, Pennsylvania

Christian Publications, Inc.
3825 Hartzdale Drive, Camp Hill, PA 17011
www.cpi-horizon.com

Faithful, biblical publishing since 1883

ISBN: 0-87509-767-7
LOC Catalog Card No.: 97-77649
© 1998 by Christian Publications, Inc.

98 99 00 01 02   5 4 3 2 1

Cover portrait by Karl Foster

I dedicate this book to my wife

Rebecca

without whose steady love I would
never have had the confidence to
either start this project or see it
through to the end.

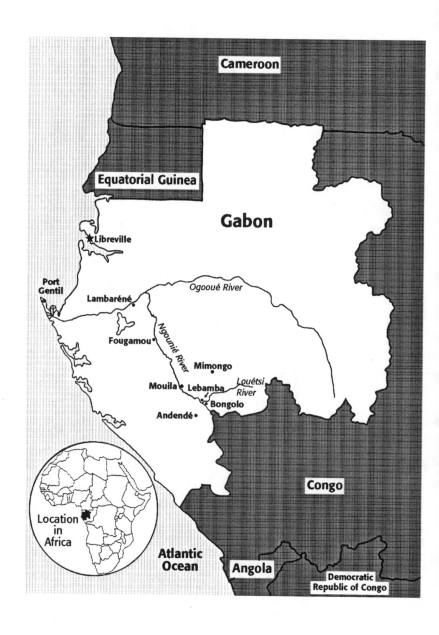

Contents

Publisher's Note

Every effort has been made to present the facts of this story as accurately as possible. The author's sources during his five years of research included official and personal correspondence, archival materials, two theses and numerous secular and religious books, plus interviews with and input from various members of the Fairley family and missionary and national colleagues. A complete bibliography accompanies the original version of this book, a history of the work of The Christian and Missionary Alliance in Gabon entitled *Beyond the Mist: The Story of God's Love for the People of Gabon*. A copy of that manuscript has been placed in the archives at the denomination's national office in Colorado Springs, Colorado.

The story you are about to read has been edited to focus on the life and work of Donald and Dorothy Fairley and certain national believers and missionaries who most directly ministered with them in service to Christ and the people of Gabon.

Introduction

When my wife and I first arrived in Gabon in 1977, we were sent to an old mission station that decades before had been carved out of the African rain forest. We were part of a medical team sent out by The Christian and Missionary Alliance to establish a hospital at the request of the Alliance Church of Gabon.

The trip inland from the capital city of Libreville took ten hours. Our medical team drove in three cars over 540 kilometers of rutted, dirt roads. As the sun settled into the trees, we came to a sudden stop. The road had disappeared into a muddy river. We watched in dismay as two Africans on the far side of the river released a rusting ferry and pulled it over to our side of the river. I thought to myself, *In fifty years, is this the best they can do?*

As the light faded, we drove our cars onto the ferry. The hull sank to within four inches of the surface of the water, but since the veteran missionaries in the lead seemed totally unconcerned, we newcomers faked nonchalance. By the time the workmen had pulled us through the swirling currents to the opposite bank, it was completely dark. In the distance, we could hear the roar of the Bongolo Falls.

The next morning, we drove down a deeply rutted dirt road to a lower hill. As the car rounded the corner and climbed onto the top of the hill, an enormous white church, flanked by four school buildings badly in need of paint, came into view. To the left sat two dilapidated buildings, looking lost in an acre of treeless, knee-high grass. They represented the dispensary that in time our team would transform into a hospital.

In the weeks and months that followed, I learned firsthand about the workings of the ram-jet pump that pushed water 200 feet from the river to a cement reservoir on top of the highest hill on the station. Using the natural power of the river, the rusting little robot had pumped continuously for over thirty years. I became only too familiar with the water-driven machinery sitting next to the falls that had spun electricity for Bongolo since 1945. I was told how two missionaries named Furman Lentz and Don Fairley had directed a crew of over 100 workers to complete the entire system of walls, dikes, reservoir, turbines and generator-house in just one year.

One Sunday morning I sat with 400 African Christians in the enormous Bongolo church.

Its lovely, open arches, elegant trusses, three-story stone steeple and flagstone floor permit believers to worship in cool and breezy comfort. When the service began, the people stood and clapped their hands in perfect unison, singing songs that were both strange and exhilarating. The music swelled and filled the church until I thought my heart would burst with delight. Looking around me, I marveled and wondered, *Who built this? Who told these people about Jesus? Who taught them the ways of God? Who wrote down their languages and translated the Scriptures for them?*

At the end of six months, I was ashamed that I had ever thought that those who preceded me could have done more. Instead, I wondered: *How in the world did they do it?*

I asked that question first to the older missionaries, then to the younger ones and finally to the older African believers who had lived in Bongolo since the beginning. Sometimes I found their stories hard to believe and privately wondered if they weren't embellishing. The oldest people talked about men and women with names like Pierson, Fairley, Klein, Cook, Shank, Ficke, Gerber, Corby, Schindler and others who had passed from the scene. They spoke their names in tones of deep respect. All of the old Africans had a special affection for one name in particular, a name they mentioned more often than all the others: Don Fairley. He was the first to come with the good news and he had stayed until he was too old to serve any longer. As I was to find out, that was not the only reason they considered him to be so special.

The years flowed into two decades and I continued to ask questions. I eventually learned that the Fairleys and the Piersons had first penetrated into the heart of Gabon on a hot, steam-driven sternwheeler dating from America's Civil War. The trip between Port Gentil on the coast and Lambaréné in the heart of Gabon took them twenty-four hours. Skimming up the Ogooué River in a sleek passenger launch powered by four 50-horsepower Yamaha outboard motors, I covered the distance in a breezy eight hours.

Along the way, I glimpsed the ruins of the mission station where a young orphan decided to walk the Jesus Way. Later, I walked in Dr. Albert Schweitzer's old hospital wards where young Paul Ndoba nearly died from typhoid fever. I stayed in the same hospital ward where George and Carol Klein mourned the death of one of their twin babies.

I stood in silent reflection outside Dr. Schweitzer's untidy study. *How in the world,* I asked myself, *how in the world did those early missionaries do what they did?*

In 1981, when my wife Becki and I returned to the United States for our first furlough, I was determined to meet Donald Fairley in person. I learned that he was living in Oregon, but it was a year before I could visit him. When I finally did, his wife Dorothy lay dying in the small room they shared at a convalescent hospital. Don was so deeply distressed by his comatose wife's condition he could think of little else. We showed him our pictures of the small hospital we had built at Bongolo, but he was too anxious about his wife to talk with us for long, returning every few minutes to Dorothy's bedside. After a brief visit, we prayed for them both and said goodbye. Dorothy Fairley died several weeks later.

By the next time I saw Don Fairley I knew a great deal more about what God had accomplished through him in Gabon. I was concerned that the story was on the verge of being lost except in its most rudimentary form. The men and women of Gabon, Europe and North America who had lived through those days between 1930 and 1960 were passing away almost daily without insuring that the letters and documents recording the birth of this important African church would be preserved and handed on to those who followed.

When in late 1989 I visited Don Fairley at a retirement home in Santa Ana, I was disheartened to learn that his mind was no longer clear. He did not know who I was and was unable to tell me anything about his life's work. In 1990, he went to be with God. I would have to rely on others to tell me the story.

There were two African men who had been
with Don Fairley from the very beginning: Paul
Ndoba and Jean Mbadinga. When I returned
to Gabon in 1990, I determined to contact
them. I spent a whole day interviewing Paul
Ndoba. He was seventy-two years old, but was
still able to add important information and
many details.

Jean Mbadinga was nearing eighty when I interviewed him for the first time. His memory
was delightfully clear. I talked with him a total
of five times and found his accounts, dates and
facts to be consistently reliable.

By early 1994 I had amassed a mountain of
historical facts and had the personal stories of
Paul Ndoba and Jean Mbadinga, two of the
three most important characters in the story I
wanted to tell. Despite repeated efforts, I was
able to find only scant information on Harold
and Ozzie Pierson, the other pioneer missionaries who opened the Bongolo work with the
Fairleys in 1935. Most of the firsthand information about the Fairleys came from the two
books they wrote (*Hunting Pygmy Hunters* and
In God's Time, God's Provision) and from others
who had worked with them or who knew them
intimately. Apart from these sanitized sources,
however, I had almost nothing that pulled the
story together or gave it emotional impact. After five years of researching I was on the verge
of abandoning the project altogether.

Then, in late 1994, I drove to Oregon and in-

terviewed the Fairleys' oldest son, Gordon.
From Gordon I was able to fill in many blanks
and get a feel for his parents' struggles at Bongolo. He promised to find out if somewhere, in
some attic, there wasn't a collection of his parents' letters and photo albums.

Several weeks later, I talked with Edia Silvis,
a former missionary to the Eshira people in
Gabon. At the end of our conversation Edia
suddenly remembered something important. In
1967 he had asked Don Fairley to describe his
missionary experiences and had recorded his
account on a reel-to-reel tape recorder. For
more than four hours, Don Fairley talked into
the microphone, describing vividly how God
had called him and Dorothy to Gabon and had
helped them establish the Church in the south.
The tape had lain virtually forgotten for twenty-
eight years!

Edia re-recorded the fragile tape onto a cas-
sette and sent it to me. I cannot describe the
emotions that surged through me as I listened
to it. At last I had Don's own account. It was
as though God had given Don Fairley permission to speak to me from the other side of the
grave.

Several weeks later, Gordon Fairley called.
One of his sisters had found a trunk in her
house filled with the Fairleys' letters, documents and photo albums. When I finished going through it, I had more than enough to tell
the story.

This, then, is the story of how an unimpressive but fearless couple and a small band of Christians penetrated a dark and awful kingdom. This is the story that God would not allow to be lost.

David C. Thompson, MD
Bongolo, Gabon
December 1995

1

The Terrors of Darkness

"Deep darkness is their morning; they make friends with the terrors of darkness." Job 24:17

No one is alive today who knows when and at whose invitation Mwiri and Bwiti came to the Great Forest, and probably few care to know how they came to rule over so vast a kingdom. To the west, the waves of the south Atlantic swept night and day over its 500 miles of shimmering beaches, hurling themselves against crumbling cliffs and tearing loose the trees from the Great Forest. For 100,000 square miles the sun's rays rarely penetrated the thick forest canopy to touch the millions of creatures living in the shadows below.

There were hundreds of varieties of trees in the Great Forest, many of them with hard,

dense woods resisting for a lifetime the wood-
bores and termites that reduced softer trees to
sawdust soon after they were felled. The older
trees loomed in the shadows like silent giants
rising on five- or six-foot trunks fifty to one
hundred feet into the air before branching out.
The peoples who eventually came to live in the
forest gave the trees names only a few ever
learned.

The Great Forest is endlessly thirsty, but to
drink, it must submit to the storm. After half a
day of bright cloudless sunshine the air becomes heavy with moisture. A stillness spreads
over the land, until even the animals and insects stop their motion and wait for the birth of
the storm they know is coming. A gentle
breeze playfully stirs the trees, then stops, as
though frightened. After a pause, a more serious wind blows, building in intensity until suddenly it tears dead leaves from the quivering
trees and hurls their lifeless branches to the
ground.

A dark cloud steals silently overhead, so gray it
seems almost blue. Another gust of wind
catches a tree by surprise and sends it shudder-
ing to its grave. The wind pauses and every living thing holds its breath. A few renegade
raindrops loosed by the blackening cloud free-
fall onto the leaves below. Then, with a shout of
thunder like an army on the rampage, the rain
roars out of the sky, advancing across the ver-
dant hills and valleys in a wall. Hours later, it

wearies of the game and slackens. But the storm is far from finished. Jagged bolts of bluish-white lightning slash down in shards of pure energy, smashing into the hapless trees, splitting and snapping the tallest and reducing the most arrogant among them to reluctant submission.

The storm eventually expends the last of its fury and subsides, having established its authority. Its rage is replaced by the pleasant sounds of the forest: water as it skips leaf by leaf to the waiting ground below; insects, reptiles, birds, animals and humans moving about once again. The drops of water melt into each other and form trickles, streams and eventually swirling rivers.

Hours later, the sun's rays pierce the thinning clouds and lighten the sky. A mist rises like incense from the trees and settles like a shroud over the land. In places it rises so thickly it distorts and finally obscures the distant mountains. Its silent whiteness makes it easy to wonder if anything at all exists—beyond the mist.

There are few forests in the world as great or as rich in wildlife, grandeur and beauty as the forest over which Mwiri and Bwiti ruled. But the gods were not the first to come.

The first people to live in the forest arrived long before. They were only about four feet tall and from the moment they arrived, the "little people," as they were referred to derisively by those who followed, loved the Great Forest. Unlike others who came later, these people were not frightened by its dark stillness and hidden dangers. Using nets made of bark, clubs, spears—and their wits—they became its masters. Their greatest hunters learned to slip under an unsuspecting elephant bull and kill him with a single thrust of the spear into the heart. For centuries they were the only humans who knew how to live in the Great Forest.

In time, war, drought and famine forced other peoples out of pleasanter lands to the north and the east to take refuge in the Great Forest. Calling themselves the Bapounou, Banzebi, Mitsogo, Massangou, Eshira, Bateke, Bavoumbou, Fang and other names, they came in successive waves, battling for territory. Deeply suspicious of each other, over centuries of intermittent warfare they eventually carved out territorial boundaries.

Although they disdained the little people, the invading tribes soon learned that the little people who appeared and disappeared in the forest like the silent mists could kill even the most powerful warrior with their tiny, poison-tipped arrows. So the invaders left them free to roam through any part of the forest they chose, regardless of the tribes' territorial claims.

The waves of migrants from the north and east brought with them the practice of ancestor worship. The high priests were called medicine men or *ngangas*, because in their roles as priests they had learned by trial and error the effects of a large variety of plants, barks and roots. They believed that if they preserved and carried the skulls and bones of their ancestors with them and appeased them, the spirits of their dead ancestors would follow them and help them.

All of the tribes believed in a continuous stream of life, that all souls remain alive and that their old life flows into the present and continues on into the future. They believed that the spirit of a dead ancestor could be reincarnated in the life of a newborn baby and live another life. They also believed in a god called Nzembi, a great, benign Creator-God. Unfortunately, he was impossible to contact and was completely silent.

Life in the Great Forest could be brutal. As the tribes penetrated deeper and deeper into the shadows, they encountered herds of easily angered elephants, wild buffalo that charged on sight and enormous herds of wild pigs. They surprised hulking, black gorillas that moved in eerie and confident silence. They found the treetops alive with bands of chimpanzees and monkeys of every description. They trembled at deadly snakes waiting high in the branches to prey on the birds in the forest canopy. When they were careless, they trod with disastrous results on others that slept or waited in the underbrush. Along the network of streams and rivers they discovered giant pythons. The successive tribes learned the hard way that the rivers and swamps teemed not only with fish, but also with crocodiles drifting invisibly in the still water with only their eyes and the tips of their snouts breaking the surface. Even more than the crocodiles, they learned to fear the silent hippopotamus who without warning over-turned their canoes and crushed those thrash-ing in the water in powerful jaws. Where there were no snakes, there were columns of blind army ants a billion strong weaving their way vo-raciously along the forest floor in lines that stretched for miles.

But the most terrifying animal of all was the leopard. The largest species, with four or five brown spots grouped on his fur like pawprints, grew to a length of eight or nine feet and some-times weighed more than 300 pounds. The sav-agery of the leopard's attack was in shocking contrast to the silence of his approach. His ra-zor-sharp claws were able to reduce a man or a woman to ribbons in seconds. In the dark of night, the leopards hunted alone or in pairs and were afraid of nothing. They disdained man-made traps, climbed trees, swam rivers and outran every animal of the forest. The greatest warrior caught alone by the leopard was virtu-ally helpless even if armed with a steel-tipped spear.

The people needed help to live in a land so forbidding, so their *ngangas* called upon their ancestors and upon the gods they knew to come to their aid. They also called on those they did not know. One who responded to their call was a spirit who identified himself to the people as "Mwiri, the Guardian of the Great Forest." Was he a god they brought from another land or was he a new spirit responding to their invitation? It did not matter. Mwiri, the Guardian of the Great Forest, answered their summons.

In time, the worship of Mwiri became more or less standardized. Knowledge was power and the older men used that knowledge to maintain their power over the younger men. The knowledge of Mwiri could only be obtained after initiation into a secret society, usually at puberty. During the initiation, the young men were required to learn and vow to obey a long list of rules and taboos. When this was complete, they were instructed to call upon Mwiri to come to take possession of their minds and their bodies. They were then taken to the forest at night and blindfolded.

In absolute silence, they waited for the dreaded Mwiri to come. They were told that when he came, he would bite them on the upper arm, drawing blood and leaving a scar that would mark them for life. While the young men waited in silent fear, the *nganga* donned a Mwiri mask. The older men chanted and sang to the pounding of the drums while the man who represented Mwiri called on the spirit to physically come into his body. When the drumming and the dance reached a crescendo, the *nganga* "became" the physical incarnation of

Mwiri. As the drums continued to pound, the incarnation of Mwiri slipped into the forest and, after finding the waiting initiates, "bit" them by slashing each one twice on the upper arm with a razor-sharp knife before fading back into the forest.

Although the people called on Mwiri often, even he seemed to have little power over the leopard. Sometimes a leopard who had acquired a taste for humans would wait until the middle of the night before entering a sleeping village. Silently, it circled the houses, smelling its prey, searching for a weak spot in the thin bark walls. It then smashed through the flimsy bark and with a roar dragged its screaming prey off to the forest to devour. Clearly, something more powerful than Mwiri was needed to protect the people from the leopard.

Legend has it that Bwiti first came to someone from either the Mitsogo or Bapingi tribe, although others dispute this. The truth is, no one knows anymore who invited him. In any case, the worship of Bwiti became inextricably linked to a drug extracted from a plant the people called *iboga*. The use of this mind-altering drug opened a door from the dark spiritual world through which Bwiti and his minions entered.

Those who used the *iboga* root soon discovered that when they chewed it they were invigorated and powerful for hours. Perhaps a medicine man experimenting to find useful herbs and plants first discovered the plant. Once discovered, it would not have taken him long to figure out that if he pounded the root he could extract its juice and drink a stupefying dose producing euphoria and mild hallucinations. As his experience with the plant grew, so would his confidence have grown, until the day he swallowed a dose so large that he fell into a coma and was carried on a tide of terrifying dreams.

Almost all of the peoples that migrated into the Great Forest believed that dreams were real experiences of the soul during sleep. To *iboga's* discoverer, the plant opened a secret door that allowed him and those with whom he shared his secret to travel into a mysterious and hidden world. It was in that hidden world of nightmares that the spirit who called himself Bwiti made himself known to the people of the Great Forest.

In one of the most vivid and consistent dreams experienced under the influence of *iboga*, initiates saw the spirits of their dead ancestors walking in a long line. The spirits seemed somehow dazed, as though in a trance. The long line of the dead stretched to an entrance where stood a creature so fearsome that one could not bear to look at it for more than a moment. The initiates described the creature they saw as emaciated, almost decaying. Its flat, pale face had horizontal slits for eyes and a nondescript hole for a mouth. The creature directed the line of dead spirits through a door that led into blackness.

The guardian to the place of the dead revealed to the travelers that he was called Bwiti. For centuries, the *ngangas* had known how to call familiar spirits to appear and when they called on Bwiti by name, he appeared. They soon discovered that the spirit they had called was more powerful than any spirit they had ever known.

The first man to discover the effects of the *iboga* plant and to successfully invoke Bwiti held great power in his hands. Unless he was cut from a different cloth than all of the *ngangas* who followed, he did not share his knowledge until he was secure in his power and then only to those he trusted or could control.

Discovery led to experimentation and experimentation led to more discovery. Bwiti's worshipers learned that their god would materialize at their gatherings if they danced to the pounding of the drums. They learned that Bwiti was pleased when they sang or chanted songs praising his power and greatness over and over until their minds were numb. These dances became known as "Bwiti dances" that only men were allowed to attend. A woman or a child who was caught watching would be instantly put to death. The dances were held in the forest or in an enclosed "Bwiti house." Because Bwiti made it known that he hated the light, the dances could only be held at night. Dancing frenetically to the beat of drums for hours at a time without stopping, the men fortified themselves periodically with *iboga*. Entranced, spinning and jerking, they danced until they resembled the spirit they worshiped, their shadows flitting grotesquely on the walls of trees and plants surrounding them.

When the *ngangas* and their followers submitted their minds and bodies to Bwiti and drank moderate quantities of *iboga*, the spirit enabled them to perform unbelievable acrobatic feats, sometimes leaping five, even six feet straight up into the air from a standing position. Men almost routinely walked on live coals without burning their feet. There were other bizarre demonstrations of superhuman power involving the reproductive organs best left undescribed. During these séances, it became commonplace for Bwiti to appear as a shimmering, pale form. When Bwiti was pleased, he gave the *ngangas* the power to perform public miracles, such as causing it to rain on only one house at a time or making tongues of fire appear in the air.

As a result of Bwiti's spectacular demonstrations of power, more and more villages entered his embrace. Neighboring chiefs and *ngangas* feared what Bwiti might be induced to do to them. They quickly sent envoys bearing gifts to find out who Bwiti was and how they could become part of the Secret Society of Bwiti.

As with the worship of Mwiri, in time the worship of Bwiti became organized to assure the ascendancy of the men who knew its secrets. The knowledge of Bwiti and of *iboga* could only be learned if one was initiated into the secret society.

After most or all of the full-grown men were inducted into the society, the initiation rites were incorporated into the rites of puberty, separate from, but not replacing, the rites of Mwiri, who remained the guardian of the forest. Once a year the organizers built a hut of leaves large enough to accommodate the candidates from several neighboring villages at a secret place in the forest.

On a day chosen by the most powerful *nganga*, or Bwitist, as he became known, the initiates were taken to the initiation house and circumcised. They were then instructed to drink three full bowls of *iboga* brew. The brew was bitter and, if the initiate vomited, he was required to retake the dose. Soon after drinking the *iboga*, the initiates lapsed into a coma that lasted for two to three days. Most of the young men emerged weak and exhausted, but occasionally one or two awakened in a state of mental imbalance that persisted for the rest of their lives. When this happened, they and their parents were looked upon with scorn.

After regaining their strength and healing from their circumcision, the young men were interviewed by the mature Bwitists to determine if they had seen Bwiti, either in the Place of the Dead or elsewhere. If not, they had to repeat the process or remain excluded from the Bwiti secret society.

The worship of Bwiti spread from village to village and finally from tribe to tribe, until virtually all of the tribes of Gabon had embraced this new god. As decades passed, more and more men came to know Bwiti only too intimately. In fulfilling his increasingly bizarre demands, they advanced in power, success and prestige in their communities. All the while, they believed that they were the manipulators of a great spiritual power that would render them virtually invincible.

Bwiti's first demand was relatively simple: to be worshiped in dance and song, preferably under the influence of *iboga* to the point that for brief periods of time he completely controlled the people's thoughts, emotions and bodies. The second demand was that he be given free access to his followers' minds. The third was that the worship leader dress and paint himself to emulate Bwiti's ghastly appearance. This required the leader to make and wear a mask that resembled Bwiti. To simulate the shimmering undulations of the spirit, the medicine man wore a costume made with long, dried grass. To complete the effect, he smeared his arms and legs with a white clay. These were the rituals that became necessary to invoke Bwiti and to obtain his supernatural power and protection.

Few men can resist the opportunity to receive undeserved power and prestige. It was only a matter of time before the Bwitists came to the belief that the wisdom and power of another man resided in the organs of his body, such as his heart or liver, and that the other man's attributes of power could be assimilated by whoever ate the dead man's organs. Ritual autopsy to determine if a person had died from the sorcery practiced by an enemy was already widely practiced. The most conclusive evidence that a death was caused by sorcery was thought to be the presence of a thin white tissue starting behind the stomach and running along the esophagus. It most certainly represented a normal anatomical structure, but since preconceptions determine the outcome of human reasoning, the presence of this white line became irrefutable evidence that murder by sorcery had been committed. Since anybody could use sorcery against an enemy, most deaths were considered to be the result of murder by sorcery.

When a Bwitist died, however, the ritual autopsy was performed with a different twist. The *nganga* took the dead Bwitist's body into the forest as soon as it grew dark and, with the help of the leading village Bwitists, sliced the cadaver open in the flickering light of a torch. Witnesses to this practice described a gruesome ritual. Cutting out the heart and liver of their fallen comrade, the Bwitists devoured the organs raw. That was only a precursor of what was to come.

The belief that the knowledge and power of

another could be had by eating his flesh led to the practice of ritual cannibalism. Hungering for more power, the Bwitists conspired to murder and eat the most powerful and knowledgeable people of their neighboring communities. When they had eaten the heart, liver and other organs, they took the skull and long bones of their victims and buried them under their beds, thus ensuring that they would retain control over the soul of the man or woman they had murdered. That soul then became the murderer's "soul slave." All of the intelligence, wisdom and knowledge of the victim now belonged to his murderer. The Bwitists believed that the souls they enslaved in this manner could be sent "out of body" to eavesdrop or even kill an enemy through a wild animal. Within a short period of time, the belief that animal attacks on people were caused by a Bwitist's soul slave became prevalent. To demonstrate that they had killed and eaten others and were willing to do it whenever it pleased them, the Bwitists filed their front teeth to sharp points. Each time they smiled, they struck fear into the hearts of their enemies.

In the late 1920s a French colonial governor tried to collect taxes in the villages of the Mitsogo people. The Mitsogo chiefs responded by giving the governor the gifts he asked for. In the culture of Central Africa, it is customary to give a gift in return after receiving one. The governor unwisely chose to ignore this custom. When he forced the chiefs to pay taxes a second time, they became angry and refused. The governor arrested several of the chiefs and led them away in chains. The Bwitists responded by surrounding the administrator's house one night and setting it on fire. When he ran out of the house to escape the fire, the men killed him with spears, carried his body into the forest and ate it. French troops searched in vain for his remains, unaware that his bones were buried under numerous Mitsogo beds.

The requirement for receiving the greatest power in Bwiti's secret society was the most terrible: A man had to kill a member of his own family as a human sacrifice. Parts from the body could then be dried and made into powerful fetishes that the murderer could wear in a secret leather pouch. Because murdering a member of the village or of the clan was considered by all to be a crime punishable by death, it took considerable skill and forethought. Someone finally came up with the idea to kill his victim and blame a leopard. Wearing iron claws fashioned in village kilns, "leopard-men" began to prey on lone women and children, usually at night. The victims' bodies were found slashed and horribly mutilated with claw marks. Death could now come from one's own family.

Perhaps the most dramatic demonstration of the Bwiti's power occurred when a great Bwi-

tist died. It was accepted by all that Bwiti's and
Mwiri's power did not extend over death. Neither had ever succeeded in bringing someone
back to life from the dead. Bwiti obscured that
failure by staging a spectacular miracle during
a Bwitist's funeral. When a great Bwitist lay dying, he could request to be carried to his grave,
not by his fellowmen, but by Bwiti himself.

After the grisly ritual autopsy in the forest on
the night that followed his death, what remained of the dead man's body was sewn shut
with bark twine and returned to the village. Instead of taking the body back to the customary
mourning place in the kitchen, the village Bwitists placed the body on a mat or low bed in
front of the house. The women and children
were shut inside their houses. The drummers
were called, the dancing and singing began,
and *iboga* and palm wine were liberally passed
around. Eyewitnesses described the following
scene.

As the tempo of the drums increases, the men
dance, encircling the body. They sing and chant
in unison, calling on Bwiti to come and carry the
body to the grave. The singing and dancing last
for hours, but the men show no signs of fatigue.
Suddenly, the pitch of the drums changes and
the air becomes electric. As though on cue, the
dancers turn toward the lifeless body and without touching it, extend their hands. The body
stirs, then stiffly rises, lifted by an invisible
power that seems to emanate from the dancers'

hands. Holding their fingers inches from the body, the men move trancelike down the torchlit path leading to the cemetery some fifty yards from the village. Supported by nothing visible, the body moves through the village and down the path between the two rows of men, floating in the air until the group stands at the foot of the open grave.

What follows is impossible to attribute to anything but the supernatural. The drums pound with new intensity. Waving their hands rhythmically toward the dead man's head, the Bwitists stand the body upright. With every change in position the drums renew their intensity. Still suspended in the air, the body turns until its back is to the grave. With one final, almost unbearable paroxysm of the drums, the Bwitists lower the body until it hovers parallel to the ground. Hands still extended, the men at last lower the body into the grave until it settles firmly on the bottom. When it is over, the exhausted pallbearers barely manage to stagger back to the village before falling onto their mats. It will take days for them to recover.

Did it not occur to the Bwitists that they and their enemies worshiped the same Bwiti? Could Bwiti not just as well inspire their enemy to kill and eat them instead of the other way around? If it occurred to them, it was by this time too late. To protect themselves from what they feared the most, they had invited a strange god to inhabit their minds and bodies.

In so doing, the people and their leaders had opened wide the gate to a creature infinitely more terrifying than the leopard. In all of the Great Forest there were now no greater powers than Bwiti and Mwiri.

As more tribes invited Bwiti into their midst, his power over the Great Forest grew. And the more powerful he grew, the more he drew his subjects into a net of depravity and evil. The people looked to Bwiti to explain to them the causes of illness and misfortune.

When in a short period of time illness visited several members of a family, the leader of the family consulted the *nganga*. He came to the house, and after asking a series of mysterious questions, searched the house for places where an evil spirit could enter. He invariably found an opening where a wall joined the roof or where there was a crack in the bark through which the offending spirit had entered.

The *nganga* then consulted the spirits to find who had sent the spirit that had eaten or destroyed the sick person's soul. It was always the same: The culprit was a close friend or family member. A father, grandfather, aunt or uncle had "eaten" part of the victim's spirit during the night in a voluntary or involuntary out-of-body experience. Since a person's soul was thought to travel during his dreams, this did not seem unreasonable.

Protestations of innocence by the accused

were useless. If the family member was loved
and respected, it was considered an involuntary
offense and, after being paid his fee, the
nganga would make a collection of odds and
ends from animal parts, plants of the forest and
other significant objects and wrap them in a
piece of animal skin or a gourd. This was called
"protection" or a "fetish" and was placed either
in the house at the opening where the offending spirit had entered or buried in a bedroom.

If, however, a prized child or someone important had died, it was a more serious matter. After the ritual autopsy, the family or the *nganga*
could demand a trial by divination, followed by
a public execution of the one who had alleg-
edly committed murder. To protect himself
from accusations of partiality if the ritual
autopsy was not considered sufficiently deci-
sive, the *nganga* often performed a long and
mysterious ceremony that ended when he
pointed out one or two possible perpetrators.

In reality, one or both of the accused were
selected because they were unpopular or had
offended the chief, the *nganga* or the village
elders in some unrelated way. Sometimes a
nganga would accuse a man and dispose of him
simply because he wanted the man's wife for
himself.

The *ngangas* knew how to mix various herbal
potions and, when an execution was called for,
would prepare a deadly poison. At the last minute it was easy to slip into one of the bowls of

poison a pinch of something that provoked vomiting. The person who vomited the poison lived, while the one who did not vomit went into a coma and died. In this way the cleverest *ngangas* appeared to be impartial and made it seem like Bwiti had executed the guilty person and allowed the innocent person to live.

Some *ngangas* befriended the secretive Pygmies and learned from them how to make the deadliest poison of all from the seeds of the strophanthus plant.

When the *nganga* wanted to use the strophanthus poison in a trial, everyone in the village was called to witness the event and the accused person was given all the palm wine he wanted. The *nganga* then prepared a harmless brew and told the people that it would only kill someone if he were guilty as charged. When the accused was feeling relaxed from the palm wine, the *nganga* led him into the darkened Bwiti house and, after rubbing strophanthus on his palms, took a sharp knife and made several long, mysterious incisions over the forearms of the accused. He then rubbed his palms over the bleeding cuts. Next, the *nganga* led the accused out of the Bwiti house and into the center of the crowd.

In full view of the entire village he poured into two bowls the harmless brew he had prepared, drank the contents of one bowl and gave the other bowl to the accused. Confident of his innocence and of the fairness of the trial, the accused drained the contents of his bowl. Within a few minutes, the poison that had been rubbed into the cuts on his forearms took effect and the accused fell to the ground. He would be dead within minutes, confirming to even his dearest friends that he was indeed guilty of killing another by devouring his spirit.

Within several decades, Bwiti had succeeded in destroying love and trust between spouses, between parents and their children, between grandparents and their grandchildren and between close friends. Families, clans, even whole villages were divided in fear and bitterness over mostly false accusations. Bwiti did more to destroy the sense of community than did any other factor or combination of factors. Bwiti held the people of the Great Forest in an increasingly cruel and tightening grip.

As the years under Bwiti blurred into centuries, a single word came to describe the day-to-day existence of the several hundred thousand people enslaved in the Great Forest: fear. They were surrounded by a hostile environment, preyed upon by terrifying animals and through sorcery stalked by the members of their own families. Some began to secretly wonder if their gods had deceived them. Most of them would never know until it was too late.

2

A Tale of Three Men

"I was found by those who did not seek me."
Isaiah 65:1

In about 1914 a young African woman named Divagu gave birth to a male child in a tiny village. He was her third child. The birth was difficult because the child was big and because two months prior to his delivery the boy's father had thrown his mother out of the house.

Mbadinga was barely walking when he first became aware of the drums pounding at night. Sometimes he could hear voices shouting. The sounds both fascinated and frightened him. At other times, the whole village danced, the women on one side, the men on the other. There were many kinds of dances, but the Bwiti dances that went on all night long in the Bwiti house or in the nearby forest were the most frightening.

When he was six years old Mbadinga's mother took him to see a *nganga*. The *nganga* dressed him in an antelope skin, tied a number of fetishes to his body and, after calling on Bwiti, presented the boy to the spirit to guard him.

Some months later, Mbadinga was playing with his machete in front of his house one morning when, to his surprise, six men from the village where his mother lived arrived, carrying his mother into the house on a mat. He stood as they went past him, then went back to his play until the men emerged from his house.

"Mbadinga," one of them said, "your mother is dead."

"She is not!" Mbadinga replied indignantly. "I just saw her. She is sleeping!"

In a moment, the courtyard was filled with weeping relatives, throwing dirt on themselves, rolling on the ground and beating themselves with their fists. Mbadinga ran inside the house and fell on his mother, but her body was cold and she did not respond to his cries. His brother finally dragged him away. The next morning they wrapped his mother's body in a mat and buried her in the village cemetery fifty yards away from the edge of the village. Mbadinga was taken the next day to live with his Uncle Moukaga.

Soon after, Mbadinga's life took a definite turn for the worse. His uncle had always been especially attentive to Mbadinga, but some time later he heard there was work on the coast and left, promising to return after several months with money, tools for gardening, blankets and clothing.

After Moukaga left, his wives treated Mbadinga like a slave, requiring him to do twice as much work as their own children, giving him only leftovers to eat, failing to inspect his feet for the tiny insects called "jiggers" that embedded themselves under the toenails, and generally neglecting him. Within four months of his mother's death, Mbadinga developed numerous raised, red sores on his arms and legs and a common fungal infection spread through his hair causing round, bald patches to appear. Thin and dirty, too weak to do anything but lie on his mat in his darkened room or stumble into the nearby forest to relieve himself, Mbadinga's life flowed out of him like the drainage ebbing from his sores. The jiggers multiplied and covered his feet with little abscesses until he could no longer walk from the pain.

If a family friend had not seen Mbadinga's condition and gone to the coast to tell Moukaga, Mbadinga would surely have perished. To Moukaga's credit, he left his work and hurried home, walking for several days through the forest. When he arrived and saw Mbadinga's condition, he picked the boy up in his arms and wept. Then he tenderly carried little Mbadinga to the river where he washed him, shaved his head and dressed his sores with herbs. He took a sharpened stick and one by one dug out the hundreds of jiggers in Mbadinga's feet, then washed and covered the bloody flesh with a dressing of leaves.

Mbadinga's brother Divungui heard that his little brother was dying and hurried home from Lambaréné where he had found work in a sawmill. Like his uncle, he too wept when he saw Mbadinga's condition. For the next several weeks he and Moukaga nursed Mbadinga back to health. The boy never forgot Moukaga's tears and from that moment on loved him like the father he had never known.

While he was home caring for Mbadinga, Divungui suggested to Moukaga that Mbadinga return to Lambaréné with him to go to school at the Catholic Mission. But Moukaga wanted Mbadinga to grow up in the village to learn the secrets of Bwiti so that he could protect the family. He refused to let Mbadinga go.

Mbadinga, however, had been enthralled by the things Divungui had described. He determined that, no matter what, he would escape to the Catholic school. His every private conversation with Divungui ended with the same desperate plea: "Take me with you when you go back!" But Divungui returned without him.

Then one day, Mbadinga heard that Boukasa, his uncle's son, was planning to go to Lambaréné. For days Mbadinga cried and pleaded to go along. Finally, unable to bear it any longer, Boukasa gave in to Mbadinga on the condition that they leave secretly on a moonless night and that the boy promise not to whine when he got tired. Mbadinga was so excited he could hardly keep from dancing as he did his chores.

For the next few days the boys hid food in a secret place in the forest. Several nights later around 2 a.m. Boukasa woke Mbadinga with a gentle kick in the ribs. The two boys stealthily rolled up their mats, slipped out the door of the house and headed down the shadowy path. They stopped long enough to fill their shoulder bags with the food they had hidden, then ran until they were breathless. Afraid that his father would pursue them and punish him, Boukasa insisted they walk all night and all the next day, stopping only to drink at streams and eat some of the food they carried. That first night and day they walked for seventeen hours and, although Mbadinga's feet swelled to twice their normal size, he did not complain.

Some ten days later, after walking over eighty kilometers through some of the wildest country in Gabon, they finally arrived in Lambaréné. If they were to eat, Boukasa would have to find a paying job. There were more than twenty well-built houses in Lambaréné in which colonial officials, missionaries and businessmen lived, so he went from door-to-door asking if anyone wanted to hire a "boy." Mbadinga trailed along behind, getting hungrier and wearier as the day

wore on. They finally arrived at the house of a
man named Fanganovani.

Fanganovani was an unusual man for three
reasons: He owned a logging business and sawmill in Lambaréné; he was a successful African
of the Galois tribe at a time when most successful businessmen in the interior of Africa
were Frenchmen; and he was an enthusiastic
Protestant Christian.

The Fanganovani house was quite large,
painted white and made of hardwood. There
were tended gardens with bright flowers and a
clean walkway leading to the front door. Mbadinga felt out of place. As Boukasa, coughed
loudly at the door, Mbadinga tried to appear as
small as possible on the path behind him.

A moment later, the largest woman Mbadinga had ever seen emerged from the open
door. She greeted Boukasa and listened with
pursed lips as he asked in broken French if she
needed a worker. Something about the figure
behind Boukasa caught her attention. Although Boukasa continued to talk, Mrs. Fanganovani's eyes turned toward the small boy
wearing nothing but a ragged loincloth. The
long walk had melted away every ounce of
body fat and his collarbones and ribs stood out
sharply. His hair had turned brownish-red from
lack of protein and his thin little legs looked
barely able to hold up the swollen belly above
them. He was the most pathetic and appealing
child she had ever seen. Although she had

eight children of her own, Mrs. Fanganovani's soft heart melted on the spot.

The year was 1919, give or take a year, and although Bwiti didn't know it yet, Mbadinga had just escaped from his claws into the ample bosom of Mrs. Fanganovani.

Mrs. Fanganovani's wonderful cooking soon filled out Mbadinga's spindly legs and turned his coppery hair a luxurious black. As his body filled out, his head took on normal proportions and his features softened. Mrs. Fanganovani gave him clothes, taught him how to wash with soap and clean his teeth with a stick. As Mbadinga learned the rules of the house and diligently did his chores, the other children stopped making fun of him and began to treat him like he belonged. In time, he almost became a member of the family.

Because the Fanganovanis were of the Galois tribe, Mbadinga at first could not understand them. He was a quick learner though and within six months could converse fluently.

Mbadinga learned that the Fanganovanis called themselves Protestants. He had heard from the Catholic children near his village that Protestants were terrible people who lied and cheated and who were to be avoided at all costs. But the Fanganovanis were kind and gentle people. Soon after he arrived they gave Mbadinga a French name—Jean. His full name was now Mbadinga Jean.

When Mbadinga was eleven years old, his

brother Divungui came to visit him, something
he did several times a year. Divungui was
twenty-one now, but he was more than just
older. As the brothers talked, Mbadinga
learned that his brother had been initiated into
the Bwiti Society. As much as Mbadinga pried,
Divungui refused to talk about it.

"Don't you understand anything?" he shouted
at Mbadinga. "To divulge secrets about the
rites is to die!" Sensing that his brother's interest was more than curiosity, he added gruffly,
"This thing that I have done is not for you. I
want you instead to go to the Protestant school
in Ngomo and learn to read and write." And so
Mbadinga's future was decided. He packed his
few clothes and belongings in a basket that the
Fanganovanis gave him, said goodbye to his
adopted family and the next day left with Divungui in a canoe headed for Ngomo.

The Ngomo mission and school had been
carved out of the jungle on the banks of the
Ogooué River beginning in 1898. In the inter-
vening years, the missionaries had built several magnificent, two-story, burnt-brick
school buildings, a dispensary, a large church
and numerous permanent houses. When
Mbadinga and Divungui pulled up to the
shore there were no children in sight, only a
group of women.

Divungui led Mbadinga along the path to the
main school buildings. Mbadinga stared

through the open windows at the rows and rows of boys reciting after their teachers. When Divungui asked a woman where the director's office was, she pointed to a door in the center of the ground floor of the largest building. The boys stepped up onto the veranda and Divungui cleared his throat loudly.

A thin, bespectacled Frenchman stepped out of the door. His white pants, white shirt and scuffed white shoes had seen better days. When he saw the two boys he smiled, extended his hand, introduced himself as Pastor Soubéran, and asked Divungui what they wanted. Divungui hesitated a moment, then pointed to Mbadinga.

"This is my brother. I want you to take him."

"As what?" the pastor asked, knowing the answer already.

"As a student! I can pay for him."

"School began two months ago," the pastor said, his eyebrows raised. "It's late for him to start school now. Besides, we're already full for this year. Where are you from?"

"Moabi," Divungui replied hopefully.

"That is in the south, is it not?" asked the pastor. When Divungui nodded, the pastor asked, "What tribe are you from?"

"We are Bapounous," he said proudly. Pastor Soubéran did not reply for a moment, but looked from one to the other several times. Finally he turned and motioned for the boys to come into the office.

"We have no Bapounou students here and never have. There are too many languages in the south. Does the boy speak French?"

"He speaks Omyéné," Divungui replied as Mbadinga stood next to his chair. "But he is very bright. He can learn French quickly." It was clear that the pastor was very interested.

"I would like to have someone from the Bapounou tribe here in our school," Soubéran responded. "If the boy is willing to keep all the rules and to study hard, I will keep him for you." Divungui smiled in relief. Mbadinga could see that things were going as his brother had hoped. He stared out the window, hiding his disappointment while the pastor and Divungui talked about the school fees and Divungui paid for the first semester. By the time they finished, school was out for the day and they could hardly hear for the noise of 400 boys talking, shouting, running and laughing all around them. Pastor Soubéran took them to a dormitory and assigned a bed to Mbadinga. It was November 1925.

For five hours the rain poured out of the night skies, until even the mightiest of the trees bowed under its weight. The small cluster of thatch and bark houses huddled in the clearing below trembled with each gust of wind, leaking rivulets of water onto those trying to sleep. In one house, however, everyone was awake. A large, muscular woman had been in labor since the previous day and the three women helping her were almost as weary as she. This was her eighth child. Only months before, her husband and several of her other children had died. Would any of her children grow to adulthood?

As another contraction tensed her abdomen, the other women urged her to push. Grasping her ankles with her hands, she leaned back against her friend, took a deep breath and pushed until the veins on her face and neck distended and her face darkened. When she began to see spots before her eyes, she relented and gasped for air. Less than ten minutes later, her child was born. It was another boy.

As the women with her tied the baby's cord with a piece of homemade twine and cut it with a sharp knife, she lay back on her mat in exhaustion. In the flickering light of the fire, the women passed the baby around and examined him carefully for deformities. Seeing none, they wrapped him in a clean cloth and laid him in his mother's arms. Both slept until the rain stopped and the first rays of sun filtered through the morning mist.

The year was 1918. The small collection of houses was part of the village of Fougamou, inhabited by members of the Eshira tribe. The village was built on a long, gentle hill, surrounded by higher forest-covered mountains. Toward one end of the village lay an odd col-

lection of large, gray boulders, several of which
stood over ten feet high.

As smoke from the newly kindled kitchen
fires filtered through the thatch roofs and hung
in the damp air, relatives arrived to see the new
baby and congratulate his mother. To each
group the mother explained with little emotion
the name she had chosen for her baby: "This
man-child is just an added deception to the
many I have already known. He is born to die
like my other children. His name is Ndoba."
She did not have to explain further why she
had chosen a name that meant "deception." It
was not a promising beginning.

Ndoba's uncle was Kengélé, the most important chief in the Fougamou area. But Ndoba's
mother was a widow. Without a husband to
hunt meat or bring home fish, to rebuild the
house or to clear trees for new plantations,
Ndoba's family slid inexorably into poverty.
When Ndoba was two he was weaned from his
mother's breast to begin eating adult food. This
was always a critical time in a child's life. Full
immunity to malaria did not develop until age
six or seven and, like other children his age,
Ndoba had week-long bouts of malaria fever at
least once a month, leaving him chronically
anemic and always on the edge of malnutrition.
In addition, everyone was infested to some de-
gree with intestinal parasites, but children
Ndoba's age could afford it the least. If a

three- or four-year-old child developed diarrhea or two consecutive bouts of malaria in one month, the balance was almost always tipped toward kwashiorkor (severe protein malnutrition) and death. To almost everyone's surprise, Ndoba survived this period of his life.

Ndoba's mother remarried and became pregnant with her ninth child. Soon after, she died, leaving Ndoba an orphan. As was customary, Ndoba's Uncle Kengélé brought him to live in the house of one of his wives. Even though he took responsibility for Ndoba, it was up to his wives to care for the boy and feed him. But in a household with more than thirty children, Ndoba was all but forgotten. His daily ration amounted to a single ear of roasted corn. Unloved and unwanted by women who had enough work feeding and caring for their own children, Ndoba was left alone in the village when the women went with their children to work in the fields. It mattered little to anyone whether he lived or died.

By some strange providence, Ndoba did not die. Instead, he began foraging on his own to find food in the forest, eating whatever fruit on bushes and trees he could find that was edible and making traps to catch small animals and fish. While others lived on the food grown by their mothers and hunted and fished for fun, Ndoba learned to survive by his wits and hard work and to prepare food and cook for himself.

About this time a Catholic priest came to

visit Ndoba's village. He had built a house and a church at a settlement called Sindara some twenty kilometers downriver. He taught the people about the Creator-God, about the first people in the world called Adam and Eve, about sin and God's anger and about someone named Jesus Christ who had been brutally killed when His enemies had nailed Him on a tree. The priest told the people that they were God's enemies, but that they could become His friends and children if they burned their fetishes, abandoned the worship of Bwiti and Mwiri, were baptized as Catholics and followed his teaching.

The priest spoke and acted with such authority and confidence that the people assumed he was authorized by the colonial government to do whatever he wished in their villages. They knew how the French rulers had crushed all resistance in the past and so were afraid to openly oppose the priest. They had heard that in other areas when people ignored them, the priests had burned down their worship houses and had gone house-to-house searching for fetishes and burning them.

Kengélé did not want trouble with the French rulers. He also knew that if the priest opened a school in his area, his children would learn to speak French. So Kengélé instructed his people to cooperate.

Ndoba was among the first group of students to enter the school. Ndoba had escaped death.

And because of the priest and his school, Ndoba also had escaped being initiated into the Secret Society of Bwiti.

On November 26, 1905 in Zion, Illinois, a little boy was born. His name was Donald Archibald Fairley. Had his father not been soundly converted to Christ while studying for the British Foreign Service at the University of Edinburgh, Donald would have been born in Scotland into an upper-middle-class Scottish family. His father's conversion so changed his worldview that he abandoned his studies and became a minister of the gospel. In 1900, at the age of thirty, he sailed for America. Several years later, Archibald fell in love with a young woman named Emma Ellison who was touring with a Canadian choir. She had grown up in St. Thomas, Ontario and was a gifted musician and artist.

The Fairley family lived in Chicago, Illinois until Donald was fifteen years old. By this time he had demonstrated unusual intelligence and an almost uncanny ability to do anything he put his mind to do. Already he could cook, build, fix almost anything mechanical or electrical, raise bees, garden and drive a car. While others complained that there was no work to be found, Donald had a keen eye for hidden opportunity, somehow always finding a way to earn money. He had one other interest that he had gotten from his parents that set him apart from his friends and schoolmates—he was fascinated with animals, especially wild animals.

In 1920, Donald's father decided to take a pastorate in Oregon. Leaving his family behind, he went ahead to find a house for them. A few months later, fifteen-year-old Donald drove his mother, brother and two sisters from Illinois to Oregon in the family car.

The following year, after completing his junior year in high school, Don announced to his astonished parents that he was going to Alaska for the summer to earn money at a salmon canning factory in Ketchikan. Against their wishes, he purchased a train ticket to Seattle. The first night, he was robbed of his watch, a pistol he had brought for his protection and all but $2 of his hard-earned money.

By the time Don arrived at the dock to sign up for work, the companies had hired all the white men they could use and were hiring only Asians and East Indians. Don got in line anyway. A Chinese man was giving out tickets to board a ship. When his turn came, Don reached out for a ticket and grabbed it as the man protested that " 'Melican boy no good, no workee!" Don replied, "This 'Melican boy workee plenty good!" He ran onto the ship before anyone could stop him and was directed down into the hold where he was assigned a bunk in a tier of six. As far as Don could tell, he was the only white boy on the boat.

Unhappy that they would have to share their

quarters with a member of the arrogant white race, the Chinese and Filipino workers took immediate offense at Don's presence. And what's more, the food was terrible. Don volunteered to help in the kitchen. By the end of the day his friendliness, hard work and obvious cooking skill surprised everyone. The food and the service improved and by the end of the second day he had won the respect of his fellow travelers.

At 2 a.m. on the third day the ship docked at Ketchikan for refueling. By this time Don had learned from the crewmen that the living conditions at the factory in Nome were harsh and that the work paid little. So, in the early morning hours, he took his duffel bag, crept up the ladder inside one of the smokestacks, climbed over the top and down the outside onto the deserted deck. He threw his duffel bag onto the dock four or five feet below, then jumped over the railing after it. He landed so forcefully he knocked the wind out of himself but managed, nevertheless, to run behind the nearest warehouse without being detected.

When Don showed up at the Naket Packing Corporation in Ketchikan, the salmon were running and the plant was in full operation. He explained his situation to the manager. The man took an immediate liking to him and agreed to hire him and reimburse the company he had abandoned when he jumped ship. He assigned Don to live with about sixty Filipino workers in a dormitory built on pilings out over the water.

Working twelve-hour shifts while the salmon swarmed up the coastal rivers to spawn, Don soon fell into a monotonous rhythm of working, eating and sleeping. Slight of build, only five-foot-eight-inches tall and the only non-Filipino, he soon realized he would have to survive by his wits. With his earnings he purchased a .38 special revolver and hid it under his mattress.

Don's hard work and mechanical ability caught the attention of the plant manager and at the end of July he was promoted to foreman in charge of the canning machinery. When in 1921 President Hoover visited Alaska and stopped in Ketchikan, sixteen-year-old Donald Fairley was chosen to demonstrate the canning process to the President of the United States.

During all of this time, Don thought little, if at all, about God. He had heard the plan of salvation so many times it had ceased to mean anything to him. He believed that a man was best served by hard work and an honest, moral life.

One night he and a Filipino worker got into a discussion about religion. Don became upset at some of the man's statements and the discussion escalated into a shouting match. The Filipino reached for his gun.

"Why don't you go get your gun and settle this like a man?" the bystanders taunted Don. As he headed up to his room, he heard God speaking to him as if in an audible voice.

Don Fairley, you are at a crossroads in your life. What you do now will decide if you will go up or if you will go down. It was impossible not to understand God's warning. If he continued to live for himself and without reference to God he would begin a downward slide that would eventually take him to hell. He reached under his pillow and pulled out the New Testament his father had packed in his duffel bag. The more he read, the more God spoke to him. He had been a professing Christian, had grown up in a Christian home, but now he was obsessed with making money. Closing his eyes, he prayed the prayer he had heard his father invite sinners to pray so many times before.

"God, I am a sinner. Forgive me for turning away from You. Forgive me for my many sins. Jesus, come into my life. From now on I want to live for You and to obey You."

When he opened his eyes, it was as though a great load had fallen from his shoulders. The anger that had nearly brought him to the point of killing a man melted away. In its place he felt peace and joy. He went back downstairs and, to the astonishment of the other men in the bunkhouse, made peace with the Filipino. Compared with his former behavior, his joyful manner seemed so odd that the men wondered aloud if he hadn't sampled some whiskey. The next day Don sold his gun and at the end of the summer bought a first-class ticket on the *Princess Alice* back to Seattle.

3

The Seeds of Revolution

"Your eyes will see the king in his beauty."
Isaiah 33:17

Mbadinga began his studies reluctantly. He wanted to be back in Lambaréné with his buddies attending the Catholic school. He did not like being the only Bapounou in the school and he did not like the way the other boys made fun of his tribe.

During Mbadinga's first Christmas at Ngomo, the pastor talked about how Jesus wanted to wash everyone's heart clean of sin. The thought of Jesus opening his chest and washing his heart with soap and water terrified Mbadinga. Then they sang the song, "Wash me with Your blood that was poured out for me." The imagery was too much for Mbadinga.

Even as they sang, he looked around in fear that Jesus might come for his blood. Mbadinga was bewildered and afraid of all this talk about the blood of Jesus.

The pastor noticed Mbadinga's confusion and talked to him alone, explaining how Jesus had died on the cross in his place. Mbadinga at last began to understand. That Christmas Day, he bowed his head and invited Jesus Christ into his heart. He was perhaps the first Bapounou in Gabon ever to do so.

Several months later, he presented himself to the Ngomo church leaders and asked to be baptized. He had learned the catechism and was confident that he could give all the right answers to the questions about faith and doctrine they usually asked baptismal candidates. At the examining room he was greeted by some church elders along with Pastor Njavé and the French missionary, Pastor Soubéran, sitting on benches against the walls. As he started to enter the room, a man at the door stopped him.

"Why are you here, Mbadinga?" he asked kindly.

"I am here because I want to be baptized," Mbadinga said simply. To their surprise, Mbadinga passed their review without difficulty. He was baptized the following day.

God had won a Bapounou to Himself.

By the time Mbadinga reached the third level (tenth grade), he could both speak and write

French with ease. There were many job oppor-
tunities for young men able to speak and write
French and, as the end of the school year approached, Mbadinga and his classmates talked
about what they would do after they got their
certificates. Mbadinga decided to quit school
with some of the others and go to work in Port
Gentil. He knew he could earn good money.
Although Pastor Soubéran disagreed with his
decision and urged him to stay in school,
Mbadinga refused to listen.

"Mbadinga, God has called you and is preparing you to do something more important
than working for money," the old missionary
pleaded. Mbadinga politely nodded his head
and promised to think about what the pastor
said, but he knew he had already made up his
mind. When school ended for the year, Mbadinga went to the coast to look for a job and
play with his friends.

If Mbadinga had gotten a job in Port Gentil
he would certainly have gone far. When inde-
pendence came to the country, with his intelligence and education, he would probably
have become a leader among the Bapounous
and perhaps a rich and powerful man. But
God did not let Mbadinga go. All dry season
long Pastor Soubéran was burdened to pray
for Mbadinga and, strangely enough, Mbadinga could not find a job. Soubéran decided
to walk Port Gentil's sandy streets looking for
him. He finally found him.

"What are you doing here, Mbadinga, when God has called you to be a pastor?" he asked the surprised young man. Mbadinga refused to admit that God had called him and argued with Pastor Soubéran for hours. At last he blurted out, "Who is Jesus Christ? Why should I care about Him? Do I know Him?"

In the silence that followed, convicted by his own words, he wept in shame. The next day he returned to Ngomo and enrolled at the Paris Mission's Bible school.

After Mbadinga completed two years at the school, he accompanied some French missionaries to a new mission station farther from his own people than he had ever been in his life. But with the dream still alive, he wrote a letter to Ndoba, advising him that he wanted to join any party of missionaries entering the south. The answer would come sooner than he could hope for.

It was the law of the land that all children had to have a French first name, so, when he started school, Ndoba was given the name Faustin.

Faustin Ndoba seemed to have a talent for learning languages and within six months spoke French reasonably well. The priest constantly warned the students about a terrible group of people called Protestants, not mere humans, but demons and devils who were sent by another devil, a spirit strangely similar to

Bwiti. He and the other students were repeatedly warned to avoid Protestants lest they be deceived and their souls be forever damned in a fearful place called hell. Although he was learning how to become a good Catholic, Ndoba was disappointed that the students in his school were not being taught how to read and write.

That summer when he was home from school, Ndoba decided to run away. He walked to a nearby village where there was a store. When Ndoba asked the store owner for a job, he hired him on the spot, gave him a place to sleep and clothes to wear. Ndoba was nine years old.

He learned about a place on the Ogooué River called Lambaréné, about a white doctor named Albert Schweitzer who had built a hospital there and about the school run by the French Protestants where African children were taught to read and write. The storekeeper urged Ndoba to go to the school and offered to help him pay the expenses. Still fearful of the Protestants, Ndoba resisted the idea.

But Ndoba's longing to read and write was so strong that it finally overwhelmed his fear. The storekeeper took him to Lambaréné and presented him to the school director. When school opened the following September, Ndoba (or Faustin as he became known in the school) was enrolled in the Protestant school.

The school had a missionary director and

godly African teachers who knew the Bible. Ndoba's teacher talked about the same God and Jesus Christ as had the Catholic priest, but said almost nothing about Mary or about praying to saints. Ndoba was astonished the first time his teacher opened a Bible and read from it. He had never seen anybody but a priest do that.

Ndoba had been in school for almost two years when the class began reading the story of Joseph. When the teacher read that Joseph was rejected by his brothers and sold into slavery, Ndoba wept. When his teacher asked him why he was weeping, he refused to answer.

The following week, as the story of Joseph's unjust imprisonment and suffering unfolded, Ndoba was again overcome. He listened with amazement as the teacher read about Joseph's rise to power, his triumph over his brothers and how he forgave his brothers. *God's love for Joseph was truly amazing,* Ndoba thought to himself.

The story of Joseph changed Ndoba in ways that he could not understand. From then on, whenever his teacher talked about Jesus' sufferings and humiliation, Ndoba was overcome with emotion. Finally one day during his third year of school he turned to a group of his friends.

"I am no longer a Catholic," he said. "Do we even know what we're saying when we rattle off the catechism? The words we are hearing here

are the true words of God! This is the real
truth!" After a moment of shocked silence, his
friends burst out laughing.

Although privately Ndoba believed that Jesus
Christ was really the Creator-God, still he hesitated to become a Protestant. The following
year, as the Christmas season approached, his
teacher invited any students who wished to be
baptized to stand and openly confess their
faith in Jesus Christ. Ndoba believed, but he
was too ashamed to stand in front of his smirk-
ing friends.

Shortly after Christmas, Ndoba became ill
with a fever. The school director took him to
Dr. Schweitzer's hospital where, despite the
medicines and treatments he received, the fever would not break. At times he hallucinated,
screaming and shouting until the entire ward
was awake and upset with him. For two
months he could eat nothing but small
amounts of soup or tea. His body wasted away
until he was too weak to rise from his bed.

The more Ndoba pondered his circumstances, the more he began to think that he
could either obey God and live or he could refuse to follow Jesus and die. But why should he
matter to God? Why couldn't God just leave
him alone?

In the end, Ndoba's fear of dying won out.
One night he slipped out of the ward and
found a quiet spot. Bowing his head, Ndoba
promised God that if He spared his life he

would openly acknowledge Jesus Christ to his friends and family. But again he forgot his promise.

Several weeks later, Ndoba headed to the Ogooué River. It was the hottest time of the year and the students often swam and bathed in the river after class. Ndoba asked his best friend to come with him, but he had other plans. So Ndoba went alone. At first he splashed in the shallow water near the shore, but after a while he started looking around for something more interesting to do. On an impulse, he swam to a log about thirty feet from shore. As it continued to drift downriver, he decided to swim back to where his clothes were laying on the shore.

About ten feet from the shore and beginning to tire, he dropped his feet, confident that he would be able to touch bottom. But his feet found only deep water. Before he could take a breath, his head slipped beneath the surface. Tired from battling the river's current, he lunged for the surface, gasping and crying for help. But there was no one to hear him. Once again he sank beneath the water.

A second time he thrashed to the surface, crying out and gasping for air. But still there was no one to hear him. In a flash his life passed before his eyes and he remembered that he had not kept his promise to God. He had never intended to keep his promise and now God was ending his life! A sense of despair and hopelessness filled his heart and he ceased struggling. It was over, his life was ending. He had only to open his throat, release the little air left in his lungs and allow the water to flood in.

In that moment Ndoba heard a voice say to him, "Put up your hand." Without thinking, he obeyed. An instant later, he felt someone pushing him forward in the water. His feet touched the bottom and he exploded to the surface, gasping for air and finally falling facedown on the muddy bank. His friend was standing over him. Still trembling with fear and fatigue, Ndoba walked slowly back to his dorm. *I should have died,* he thought, *but God spared my life.*

The next day Ndoba stood in class and told his story to his teacher. He ended by saying, "From this day until the day that I die, I will be a follower of Jesus Christ." This time, not a single one of his classmates laughed. Ndoba determined to present himself for baptism at the next opportunity. It was to come much later than he thought, under circumstances he could never have imagined.

Several weeks after his near-drowning, Ndoba found part-time work as a cook for a French missionary teacher named Mademoiselle Pepin. One day he asked her, "Mademoiselle, are the missionaries always going to remain here in Lambaréné?"

"Why do you ask?" she responded. Ndoba hesitated a moment.

"Could you come and live in my village of Fougamou?"

The missionary paused.

"If you want the Mission to go to Fougamou," she finally replied, "you must take it there yourself!"

"Myself?" Ndoba replied in astonishment. "How would I do that?" Obviously, she did not understand that a young boy would never be taken seriously by the tribe's elders. Furthermore, Catholic teaching and power had become so great in the Fougamou area that any African who preached a different message would be told to keep silent. Ndoba understood more clearly than even the missionaries that in French-controlled Africa, if an unsponsored African challenged the teaching of a white Catholic priest or stood up to the nganga's power, he would be chased out of town in disgrace or killed. Until he could be backed by the authority of a white man, Ndoba would wait and hope.

Soon after, he met a Bapounou Bible school student named Jean Mbadinga. Jean shared with Ndoba his longing to return to his own people with the gospel. Despite Jean's enthusiasm, Ndoba wondered what, if anything, either of them could do to convince their people to follow Jesus.

4

Boot Camp

"He did this only to teach warfare to the descendants of the Israelites who had not had previous battle experience." Judges 3:2

A s Don began to hunger after God and desire to be used by Him, the Holy Spirit swept into his life like a wind, upending the attitudes of his young heart and tuning his thoughts to the great themes of God's own heart. During the next two years, Don became a leader among the young people in his church and led many to faith in Christ and into a deeper knowledge and love for God.

Within just a few days of Don's graduation from high school, a most significant event took place in his life. On July 4, 1924, a large group of high school students and recent graduates decided to go swimming in the Willamette

River near Springfield, Oregon. With Don were his two younger sisters.

Dorothy Millicent Knowles also went with a group of her friends to the river that day to picnic and swim. She was sixteen years old and not the least bit timid in her knee-length bathing suit. With the temperature climbing above 100 degrees, she and her friends plunged into the cool water.

As the young people swam and relaxed in the brilliant sunshine, a log drifted serenely down the river. Dorothy and her girlfriends saw it, pulled it closer to shore and climbed onto it. Several boys splashing in the water nearby saw the girls and decided to join them.

Some of the boys slipped underneath the log and playfully tipped the girls off. Three of the girls saw the boys and squealed as they fell into the water, but the fourth girl was totally surprised. When the log turned under her, she fell backward into the water without taking a breath.

Still on the shore, Don saw her disappear into the water. Seconds passed, but she did not reappear. The other girls were swimming toward the shore away from the log, oblivious to what was happening to their friend. The seconds ticked on. Still she did not reappear.

"There's a girl missing! She didn't come up! There's a girl drowning!" shouted Don. Everyone ignored him, so Don dove in, disappearing deep into the murky water. After what seemed like an eternity, seeing nothing, he surfaced and yelled again. By now over a minute had elapsed. Don realized that the current had carried the missing girl downstream. Almost in panic he swam back to shallow water and ran downriver. Plunging back into deep water, he bumped into the drowning girl. She was struggling weakly, but when she felt Don brush against her, she instinctively wrapped her arms and legs around him. For one terrifying moment, he was unable to either swim or free himself. Then, remembering his training, he brought his knee up into the girl's stomach as hard as he could. Stunned, she let go. Don circled behind her, grabbed her hair and headed for the surface.

By now, his lungs were ready to explode, his legs felt like rubber and he could not think clearly. He knew that if he did not let go of the girl he could easily drown along with her. But unreasoning stubbornness welled up in him and filled him with new strength. With one last kick, he felt his head break into the air.

He knew he had to get the girl to shore as quickly as possible. Fighting to keep them both afloat, Don noticed that the current was pulling them further downriver. Fifty feet ahead he saw a sharp bend in the river. A lone fisherman sitting on the bank spotted them and began to wade into the river. If Don could only reach the man's outstretched hand, they would be saved. If not, he reasoned, he and the unconscious girl would both be swept around the bend of the river to their doom.

Don could feel his arms and legs moving more slowly, no longer doing what he wanted them to do. The fisherman was now up to his neck in the river and could go no further. Although he stretched his hand as far out as he could reach, they were still five yards apart.

Knowing all that followed, one is tempted to wonder what would have happened had Don Fairley failed to swim that last five yards on that hot day in 1924. It is a question that tantalizes, but out of necessity the answer eludes us completely. What we do know is this: On July 4, 1924, Don Fairley and Dorothy Knowles were not swept past the outstretched hand of the old fisherman. Instead, their fingers touched, then locked and the old man pulled them with surprising strength until they were out of the current and Don's feet touched bottom. The two men dragged the unconscious girl to the bank.

A large crowd gathered around and waited breathlessly as Don performed artificial respiration. Suddenly, after about twelve minutes, Dorothy coughed. A sigh of relief rippled through the crowd. A few minutes later she was breathing on her own. Even thirty minutes later, when she was fully conscious, she was only dimly aware of the young man who stood looking down at her with an expression of immense relief on his face. Later she would learn

his name and feel embarrassed that someone
had had to rescue her. But for now she was
grateful to be alive.

Within days of rescuing Dorothy Knowles
from drowning, Don Fairley began courting
her. Soon he could think of almost nothing
else. Although she was only sixteen and he seventeen, he began thinking about marriage.
Dorothy's mother was grateful to Don for saving her daughter, but she considered her
daughter to be a child and did not appreciate
the intensity of Don's pursuit.

Don's car made it possible for him and
Dorothy to attend the First Baptist Church in
Eugene. For the next two years they were part
of a large and enthusiastic group of young
Christians discipled by Pastor Charles Dunham. During a series of meetings on the work
of the Holy Spirit, Don realized that although
in Alaska he had promised God control over
every aspect of his life, he really was not willing
to allow Christ to decide anything important,
like what he was going to do in life, where he
was going to go or who he was going to marry.

One night Pastor Dunham asked those who
wanted to obey God to come to the altar and
surrender to Him their bodies and their minds.
Don went forward, but he could not surrender
his determination to marry Dorothy. He remained at the altar, struggling with his heart
until everyone in the church had gone. Finally,

several hours later, he surrendered Dorothy to God and offered to serve Him in any capacity that God chose. When at last he opened his eyes, the only light left on in the church was a small one on the pulpit. Halfway back, in one of the pews, Pastor Dunham was waiting, having prayed for Don the entire time.

The next day Don went to Dorothy's house and told her that he had decided to go with his family to live in southern California. He also explained that he had consecrated himself to Christ and that he felt he should now break off his relationship with her until God gave him clear direction concerning their future. It sounded foolish, but it was what he had promised God.

Mrs. Knowles was visibly relieved. She had already decided that Dorothy was not going to marry until she had finished college. When Don came by to say goodbye to Dorothy the next day, he did not know if he would ever see her again.

Don Fairley was nineteen years old when he moved with his parents to Santa Barbara, California. Within a few months he found a job at the Fetherhill Ranch Zoo. There were few public zoos in the West in the 1920s and most animal collections were owned by wealthy individuals. The Featherhill Ranch Zoo, owned by the Fleischmann Yeast Company, was an unusual combination of the traditional zoo and almost circus-like animal shows. Don's love and knowledge of animals, combined with his willingness to work hard, made him an instant favorite with the owner, the caretaker and the animal trainer. Within a year Don had made himself indispensable. An animal trainer named Charlie Gardner from the Ringling Brothers' Circus took an instant liking to Don and eventually made him his apprentice.

Under Charlie's teaching, Don taught the chimpanzees to eat, dress, pound nails with a hammer, ride tricycles and drive little foot-pedaled automobiles. He trained a puma, a leopard, a black panther, orangutans, a baboon, bears and finally a young elephant from India to perform tricks that would please the crowds.

Mr. Fleischmann raised Don's salary until he was making more money than anyone else at the zoo. Don felt fulfilled, secure in the knowledge that his future as an animal handler and trainer with Mr. Fleischmann was assured.

During this time Don prayed often for Dorothy Knowles. When he felt that God had at last given His approval, Don began to write her. A year passed, and the letters between the two young people became increasingly frequent. Don made his intentions very clear in his letters and, in return, Dorothy wrote that she would marry him as soon as her parents gave their consent. Unfortunately, Mrs. Knowles was not satisfied that either Don or

Dorothy were ready for marriage. The months of writing and waiting stretched into years, with no end in sight.

In 1925 an earthquake struck the Santa Barbara area, followed by aftershocks and tremors. Don was working with his animals when the first shocks hit. Seconds later, the chauffeur for the Fleischmann estate appeared at the entrance to the zoo and yelled for everybody to get away as quickly as possible before any of the animals got loose. The atmosphere of the compound became one of terror.

Don's first thought was for the animals under his care. He felt a sense of responsibility for them and, despite the chauffeur's pleas, was not willing to leave. Seconds later, the limousine roared off down the road with all the workers of the estate and the zoo inside. Only Don remained.

He grabbed a shotgun from his office and ran to examine the cages. A black panther was hanging upside-down from the roof of his cage, snarling. But the door was secure. The leopard in a nearby cage was leaping back and forth in panic, but the cage had not been seriously damaged. The monkeys were screaming. In the bird cages, dozens of them had banged themselves on the screens and were lying on the ground stunned or dead.

Suddenly, Don heard his elephant Culver trumpeting from the stockade behind him. He picked up his small hooked stick and ran toward the enclosure. The stockade gate was still closed, but the elephant had escaped onto the road leading toward the highway. His ears spread wide in rage, his eyes red with panic, the frantic animal was pulling up five- and six-inch California oaks by their roots one after another, swinging them over his back and throwing them to the side of the road.

When Culver saw Don out of the corner of his eye, he stopped and wheeled. As the elephant lumbered toward him, Don stood perfectly still. The huge animal did not hesitate, but, as though it were in battle, rushed at the lone man in front of him. There was no place for Don to run or hide.

"In Jesus' name, shut your mouth!" Don cried in as loud a voice as he could. At the sound of his voice, the elephant stopped abruptly just ten feet from Don. The animal lowered its trunk, dropped its ears and began making the familiar squeaks of companionship elephants make to others in the herd. It drew in its breath, wrapped its trunk around Don, lifted him up into the air and, turning him upside down, lowered him gently to the ground. Still trembling with fright, Don caressed Culver's trunk and talked to him gently until the animal gradually calmed down. Then, with his stick over Culver's ear, Don guided him around and around the lot, eventually leading him back into the broken stockade.

As evening approached, Don left to feed the other animals. But once again the elephant began to tug on his chain and trumpet until his head and shoulders were wet with perspiration. Don knew he couldn't keep Culver under control for long with only a chain to restrain him. Don unchained the elephant and led him into the stable. He lay down on a pile of straw next to where the elephant stood and all during the night talked to him and stroked his trunk.

Culver became Don's friend for life. And Don's courage during the earthquake did not go unnoticed by his grateful employer.

It was the spring of 1926 when Mrs. Knowles and Dorothy came to Santa Barbara to visit the Fairleys. Within hours of their arrival, Don, now twenty-one, resumed courting Dorothy, now nineteen, where he had left off two years before. In the meantime, Dorothy had decided to become a missionary. She cared very deeply for Don, but she knew that he was happy training animals and had no plans to become a missionary. She was unable to bring herself to tell him of her plans.

One day as Don was walking home from work, he passed the open door of a church. Still wearing the clothes he wore at the zoo, he smelled strongly of the anise oil he routinely smeared on himself to tranquilize the bears during his circus act. It was a warm evening and through the open door of the darkened church he saw a black and white movie showing jungle scenes. Thinking he might see pictures of wild animals, he quietly entered and sat in the back. Instead of animals, however, he saw pictures of tribal peoples living under the most primitive conditions in the mountains of Vietnam and Laos.

As he sat transfixed, God spoke to his heart: *What is more important, your animals that live for a time and then die, or these people, whose souls live forever?* It was the first time Don had considered that people ought to be more important to him than animals. He left before the lights came on, but the film had touched him deeply. He had never considered that God might hold him personally responsible for the fate of people who had never heard of Jesus Christ.

Within a few days Don's thinking had crystallized to the point that he could no longer deny that God was telling him to become a missionary to Indochina.

He was at first reluctant to tell Dorothy, but one day as they talked, he blurted it out. Her response astonished him. She explained that she had already made plans to enter Bible school and that she had been struggling about breaking off their relationship. With that obstacle removed, Don asked Dorothy to marry him. She accepted. However, when Don approached Dorothy's parents for permission to marry their daughter, he was rebuffed. Mrs. Knowles wanted her daughter to complete her education before marrying and was unwilling to consider anything else.

By the end of August, Don and Dorothy were no longer willing to wait. On September 1, 1926, the couple slipped over to the Alliance Chapel in Santa Barbara and were quietly married without either set of parents in attendance. Don's two sisters served as witnesses.

When Emma Fairley, Don's mother, learned about the secret wedding and where the newlyweds planned to spend their honeymoon, she went to the resort and confronted the couple. Fortunately for everyone, when she got there, even she could see that Don and Dorothy were not about to unmarry themselves for anybody. Don's humble attitude and determined love for Dorothy left his mother with little to say. It is hard to believe, but Don and Dorothy and Mrs. Fairley not only made their peace, but actually enjoyed themselves during their week together!

Within a couple of weeks, Don informed his employer that he would be quitting. He and Dorothy enrolled at the Bible Institute of Los Angeles (BIOLA) to begin preparation for missionary service. The zoo's owner had spent thousands of dollars building the zoo, collecting animals and developing the acts. He was very reluctant to accept Don's resignation. He even offered to support Don overseas if he

would agree to commit some of his time to
capture wild animals and ship them to the zoo.
But Donald Fairley was no longer a captive of
his love for animals. He had instead become a
captive of Jesus Christ.

During the two years Don and Dorothy studied at BIOLA, one of their classmates invited
them to a meeting at the Glendale Christian
and Missionary Alliance Church.

The speaker was Rev. Thomas Moseley who
with his wife was home on furlough from West
China. As Moseley spoke about his work, Don
and Dorothy sensed in the Alliance a dedica-
tion for world evangelism that matched their
own. The Fairleys spent the next year studying
at the Missionary Training Institute (MTI) in
Nyack, New York (now Nyack College).

The foreign secretary of the Alliance at that
time was a godly man named Dr. Alfred C.
Snead. Midway through the Fairleys' year at
MTI, Dr. and Mrs. Snead invited Don and
Dorothy to their home for dinner. After the
meal, Dr. Snead laid out a huge floor map of
Africa and pointed out the places in which no
missionary work had ever been done. The couple was stunned at the vast areas that remained
unreached.

Pointing to equatorial Africa, Snead told
them how the Church and missionaries in the
Belgian Congo (now the Democratic Republic
of Congo) had for years prayed that a young
couple would be appointed to enter as yet

unevangelized tribes in the French Congo. While Don and Dorothy pondered this, Snead went to the kitchen to help his wife with the dishes. When he returned, he found the couple kneeling on the map.

"It looks like you're interested in Africa," Snead laughed. "In fact, your knees are over one of the unreached areas. Perhaps the Lord would have you go there." Rising to their feet, the couple continued to read the names of faraway places with strange-sounding names. Somehow they were drawn to the gentle impressions their knees had made on the map.

In October 1929, having been appointed to the unreached tribes of the French Congo, the Fairleys sailed for France to begin language study.

5

Spying Out the Land

"I will give you every place where you set your foot." Joshua 1:3

On May 11, 1931, Don Fairley made his first trip into the French Congo with a team of four Christian carriers. One of their first stops was at a Swedish Evangelical Mission station. There Don learned that the Swedish Mission had decided to enlarge its work to reach all of the French Congo. The Swedish missionaries urged Don to consider entering South Gabon.

After listening to Don's report, Harold Pierson, the director of the Alliance work in the Belgian Congo, immediately began lobbying the executive committee on his field to agree to send at least two couples into Gabon without delay. But the senior missionaries in the Belgian Congo were reticent to begin such a risky undertaking without funding. Dr. Alfred Snead and the governing board in New York concurred. Most missionary societies were recalling missionaries because of the Depression. It was not a good time to be opening new fields.

But, at the annual missionary conference held in June of 1932, the Congo missionaries fashioned a compromise: As soon as it could be arranged, veteran missionary Joseph Nicholson and young Don Fairley would make a survey trip into South Gabon. If the doors were really open into South Gabon, the Fairleys, by now a family of four with the addition of Bonnie Jeanne and Gordon, would return to the United States to raise the money needed to open a permanent station in Gabon.

On February 15, 1933, Nicholson and Fairley boarded a coastal steamer and sailed for the Gabonese coastal town of Port Gentil. The morning after their arrival in Gabon they bought tickets for an ancient, wood-burning paddle wheel steamboat called the *Adjame* that was leaving that day for Lambaréné.

One of the stops was at an old mission station called Andendé. It was situated across the river from the town of Lambaréné, about a mile downriver from the hospital Dr. Albert Schweitzer had established less than ten years before.

The news that two American missionaries

had arrived and were going to make a trip into the south spread through the African community like the wind. Ndoba heard the news and became even quieter than usual. Could this be how his people would hear about the Jesus Way? The next morning he asked Mademoiselle Pepin if he could go with the Americans on their trip since they would be traveling through his country. She agreed.

Later that day, Mr. Keller, the director of the Mission, introduced Ndoba to Nicholson and Fairley. He explained that Ndoba was an unbaptized believer and a member of the Eshira tribe. He had proven to be a reliable cook for one of their single missionary women and had asked to accompany the Americans. Nicholson and Fairley liked the boy immediately and agreed to have him serve as their cook on the trip.

Early in the morning of February 28, 1933, Nicholson and Fairley loaded their supplies, men and equipment into the Paris Mission's thirty-foot-long, steam-powered covered launch. With them were young Faustin Ndoba, Jacques Lenguillaume, who would serve as interpreter, and four African helpers. They motored upriver six hours to the settlement of Sindara and were told they would have to hire a truck to take them on to Fougamou.

The next day the party was greeted by what was left of an ancient Reo truck dating from

World War I. Its body had rusted entirely away, leaving the driver perched on a bench seat with absolutely nothing in front of him but the steering wheel, pedals and motor. A wooden platform with slatted sides formed a frame behind the driver. When the men had recovered from their initial shock, the missionaries and their helpers piled their equipment and supplies onto the truck bed and climbed aboard. A hair-raising two-hour ride brought them to Fougamou where Ndoba introduced the missionaries to Chief Kengélé, the chief of the Eshira people.

Chief Kengélé, Faustin Ndoba's uncle, had traveled some distance from his own village to represent the twenty-eight sub-chiefs of the Eshira tribe. After welcoming the missionaries to his country, he asked them why they had come. Ndoba translated Nicholson's explanation.

In response, Chief Kengélé told the missionaries that most of his people had resisted the Catholic church because the priests spoke a language in worship that only they could understand. Even worse, the priests did not marry and produce children. He took this to mean that God's blessing was not upon them. He had met the French Protestant missionaries in Lambaréné and was pleased to see that they had both wives and children. Chief Kengélé was very hopeful the Americans would establish a mission in his territory.

The missionaries decided to abandon the river and to continue their journey on to Mouila on foot. Early on the morning of March 6, as the sun's rays dispelled the morning mists, a party of nineteen men set out for Fougamou. Around noon they stopped at Chief Kengélé's own village. He again urged them to settle in his country, demonstrating his sincerity with the gift of a goat and some fruit.

Since the river had always been the road into the interior, there were no clear paths or trails over the hundred or so miles between Fougamou and Mouila. The plains gradually gave way to low, forested hills, and as they continued south, the party crossed numerous streams, small rivers and finally swamps. After wading through each swamp they had to stop, undress and pull leeches off their bodies. During the four-and-a-half-day trip, they passed through forty-eight small villages.

In one large Eshira village they observed the people honoring the mothers of twins. The missionaries learned that these women traveled periodically to neighboring villages to be praised at village feasts. These practices were in sharp contrast to the practices of the neighboring tribes who believed that twins were a curse. These tribes killed one or both twins at birth and forced their mothers to live in houses marked by banana plants and fences in front of the door. Before leaving the house these women sometimes had to daub their breasts and foreheads with white clay mixed with the remains of their dead children.

At Mouila, the missionaries paid their respects first to the colonial administrator, then to the trader in charge of the post, a man name Fôret. He had been told by his superiors in Paris to do everything possible to help the missionaries when they came through Mouila on their survey trip.

The next day the administrator stamped and signed the Americans' travel papers and conscripted about twenty carriers to accompany the party on the next leg of its journey. Explaining that he had received orders from the colonial governor to send armed guards with them, he then presented the group with two soldiers armed with rifles. The soldiers were huge, muscular men, their ears, lips and noses pierced by heavy gold rings and their bodies tattooed. They were deliberately aggressive and assertive so that the people would fear and obey them.

Don tried to explain that the soldiers would frighten the very people they wanted to befriend, but the administrator was unmoved. He pointed out that between 1915 and 1925 the Mitsogo tribe had burned down the government post in Mimongo no less than three times, once killing an administrator and eating him. White people, he said, never traveled without armed escorts in the south. Early the next morning the caravan pulled out, escorted by the burly soldiers.

After walking for two hours, they came to a large and important Mitsogo village called Ivouta. Larger-than-life carved idols stood in front of many of the houses. Strange and mysterious objects of witchcraft were everywhere. Most of the men had filed their teeth to points.

The porters set their loads on the ground and the soldiers instructed them to ask the people to bring wood to build a fire. A crowd gathered some distance away to watch as Ndoba prepared the meal. Some of the people overheard Nicholson and Fairley speaking English and immediately concluded they were traders. They indicated to the soldiers that they wanted to trade skins and ivory for the famous English cooking pots. The people made several attempts to approach the missionaries to talk with them, but to Nicholson and Fairley's dismay, the soldiers kept them away.

In the morning the missionaries finally managed to talk to the grizzled old chief. His wildly braided hair, pointed teeth and lined face made him the ugliest man either of them had ever seen. With his help, Nicholson and Fairley hired a large canoe with nine muscular paddlers and spent an entire day visiting nearby Mitsogo villages and looking for possible mission sites along the river.

Turning east into the mountains the following day, the caravan advanced deep into Mitsogo territory. Each time they passed through a village, their aggressive escorts intimidated the people and literally chased them away. The frustrated missionaries concluded that unless they could convince their escorts to leave, their mission would end in failure.

That same evening they arrived at another large Mitsogo village. It was completely deserted. Fires were still burning in the houses and there was other evidence that the people had been there only moments before. The soldiers explained that they had punished the village only a few weeks earlier. French authorities had caught the people in the middle of a cannibal feast and ritual. Some of the leaders had been imprisoned.

There was an eeriness about the empty village. Nobody felt like going to bed. The sounds of stealthy movement could be heard in the brush around them. In the dim light they began to perceive men standing at the edge of the village holding iron-tipped spears. When the fire flamed up, they saw there were many of them, their bodies painted with red and white clay, watching the visitors in silence. Eventually, the men completely encircled the party just beyond the light of the fire. Nicholson, Fairley and the rest continued to talk around the fire pretending not to notice, but Ndoba and the carriers were fearful, certain that the warriors were on the verge of killing and eating them all. The armed soldiers remained uncharacteristically quiet, holding their rifles at the ready. The missionaries, however, made a point of leaving their rifles where they lay. They had not come to kill. They had come to bring life.

Before they slept, they told the soldiers that they wanted them to return to Mouila the next day. Then they lay down in the empty village meetinghouse and slept soundly.

In the morning, the village was still deserted. A dense mist gave the houses a dreamlike appearance. The group packed up their things and headed east on a clearly marked trail. Deeper and deeper they pushed into the mountains, enveloped still by the persistent mist that muffled sounds and limited their visibility to less than thirty feet. A hundred feet above their heads, the enormous trees sealed the sky over them.

After half an hour of walking, they arrived at another Mitsogo village. The chief was pleased to see them and moments later the people stepped out of their houses and gathered around the visitors, talking excitedly. Suddenly, a figure strode out of the mist and stood like an apparition before the surprised missionaries. He was painted with white and red chalk and was tattooed over most of his body. Bands and amulets, designed to protect him from his enemies and give him spiritual power, hung around his neck, waist and arms. The crowd fell silent. Obviously, this was a feared *nganga*.

"I understand you are workers of great magic and that you have come from the god-that-travels-overhead-when-it-rains," the man said.

"Yes," Nicholson replied. "We have been sent here by Him. The God whom we have come to tell you about, to whom we belong and who is taking care of us on this trip made all of these things around us. He made the trees, the forest, the animals. He made you and He made us."

The *nganga* listened for about five minutes, but gradually grew impatient and interrupted Nicholson.

"Well," he said brusquely, "we have heard why you have come and all about your God. Now you hear about ours. I want you to see where we gain our strength, how we rule our people and how we are in touch with the unseen powers." He turned abruptly toward what was obviously a house of worship and motioned with his hand for Joe and Don to enter. They hesitated. Both understood that he was proposing that they attend a demonstration of demonic power. His camera in a bag on his shoulder, Don followed the *nganga* into the house.

It was dark inside the small bark and thatch house and when the *nganga* closed the door, it became even darker. After his eyes adjusted, Don could see long rattan boxes that he later learned held ancestral bones, skulls and dried body parts. Skins and carved objects hung from the strangely painted walls. An old woman was seated in the corner grinding sticks together with water to make red paint.

The *nganga* sat down on a low stool, picked up some odd-looking bells and began shaking them and chanting. Not certain what he should do, Don decided to take a picture. Taking his camera out of the bag, he set it on a tripod in one corner of the room. It was too dark to focus, so Don went outside, got his kerosene lantern and lit it before re-entering. This upset both the *nganga* and the old woman.

Don then peeled off a couple of inches of magnesium tape and stuck it in his hand-held flash reflector. By this time the seance had come to a complete stop. The *nganga* and woman watched until, at last, Don lit the magnesium tape. It burned with a brilliant, white-hot flash and Don snapped the camera shutter. The *nganga* and the old woman screamed and rushed from the house rubbing their eyes.

In less than a heartbeat, the friendly atmosphere evaporated. As Don stepped out of the house with his camera, the *nganga* pointed at him and shouted angrily. Don motioned for Jacques to come over and explain that the camera was not magic, but just a "memory box" that he used to help him remember the things he saw. The *nganga* calmed down somewhat, but, alarmed at the muttering crowd, Joe signaled Don that they should leave as quickly as possible.

Then, from somewhere the angry *nganga* produced a very large spear. It was such an unusual spear that Don asked if he could have it as a momento of their village. His outlandish request so baffled the *nganga* that he turned away in disgust. Joe appeared at this moment with some additional gifts and suddenly everyone focused on who could grab the most. Nicholson led the shaken carriers and Don out of the village. A large group of men from the village noticed them leaving, grabbed their spears and followed them down the trail.

As the day wore on, little by little the warriors dropped away. And hours later, the last of them disappeared. Finally, that night, the two armed soldiers reluctantly agreed to return to Mouila without the Americans. For all of them, there was a palpable sense of relief that they were leaving the territory of the feared Mitsogo.

6

The "Man Who Called Animals"

"But because my servant Caleb has a different spirit and follows me wholeheartedly, I will bring him into the land he went to, and his descendants will inherit it." Numbers 14:24

The next day the party turned south toward the Massangou people. Runners preceded the caravan from village to village, announcing that unusual white men, sent by the spirit of the storm, were soon to be arriving. The Massangous were open and friendly, their villages strikingly beautiful, large and well cared for.

Soon after their arrival in the first Massangou village, the missionaries were told that the most important chief of the Massangous wished to see them. They were taken aback to discover that the chief was not only an attractive and charming woman, but that she appeared wearing nothing but a loincloth and a few beads. She welcomed them and showed them to an empty guest house. A short while later she sent a group of twenty women to the door garbed in banana-leaf hats and dresses. With great pomp, they offered the missionaries gifts of prepared food, meat, eggs, chickens and fruit and, as a customary sign of honor and respect, presented the gifts on their knees.

After three days among the Massangou people, Jacques led the caravan southwest toward the French administrative post of Mbigou. Here they encountered the largest tribe yet— the Banzebi people. Their chief, a muscular man named Ngokelélé turned out to be as open and friendly as the Massangou people had been.

The missionaries were amazed to find carbon steel knives with sharply ground edges. The Banzebi chiefs carried intricately carved walking sticks on which each chief carved an account of his exploits before passing it on to his son. These sticks represented great authority and spiritual power and the mere presentation of a chief's stick by a messenger required immediate obedience to the messenger's orders.

The people could not understand why Nicholson and Fairley wouldn't admit that they were really traders. They spoke English like the English traders who had come fifty years before, so why weren't they interested in commerce? They did not act and speak with authority like the Catholic priests who had recently established themselves twenty kilometers to the north of Mbigou. And what on earth was a Protestant? The Americans' real purpose in coming became the subject of intense debate.

On the second day at Mbigou, the missionaries encountered a group of seven Pygmies. The little people stood only about four feet tall, their abdomens distended and oversized above tiny loincloths. They were extremely fearful and nervous in the presence of the white men. Don took out a beautiful necklace and gave it to the Pygmies, asking them to take it to their chief and requesting a meeting with him.

On the evening of the third day in Mbigou the men again sat around the fire and talked through their interpreter. Somehow they had to make these villagers understand why they had come. Despite Jacques' explanations, Chief Ngokelélé could not seem to understand that the Americans had come so far and expended so much effort simply to tell them about the Creator-God and His Son Jesus.

It grew late and most of the people left the fire, closed the doors to their bark houses and went to bed. Only the missionaries, Chief Ngokelélé, some of his elders and Jacques still sat around the low fire burning in front of the guest house.

After a minute of silence, Don cupped his hands over his nose and mouth and began to imitate a chimpanzee. He was rewarded by such looks of astonishment that he made more animal sounds, imitating the African hornbill, an elephant and finally a leopard.

The reaction blazed like a thunderbolt through the village. The men around the fire jumped to their feet and exclaimed in fear and amazement. People who had been sleeping poured out of their homes and gathered around. Ndoba was not the only one who wondered if a leopard might not suddenly appear out of the darkness.

Finally Chief Ngokelélé spoke, silencing the voices of the crowd that had quickly gathered around them.

"Now it is clear to us who you are. Now we understand why you have come to us." Pointing to Don with his carved stick, he said, "You are the spirit of a great Pygmy hunter, and a former inhabitant of this country! You are someone who died and went downriver a long ways away. You have returned to us as a white man!"

Everybody started talking again and nodding their heads in agreement. Before turning in for the night, the chief added, "Tomorrow I will ask my uncle Kumiki's personal hunting guide to lead you to the Pygmy chiefs. You will meet your own people in the forest." There was nothing more to do but go to bed and see what the next day would bring.

Early the next morning Chief Kumiki's personal hunting guide appeared at their door. The missionaries and their carriers quickly packed and set out after him.

Toward noon, the guide stopped along the trail and motioned for Don to follow him into the forest. Joe Nicholson wanted to come too, but the guide refused. Only the "Man Who Called Animals" could come. The guide led Don along a little trail that only his eyes could see. After a few moments, two little men and a youth appeared in front of them. Don noticed that the older of them was wearing the necklace he had given the Pygmies the day before. The Pygmy chief was about four feet four inches tall, with a fine face, a beard and sparkling eyes. Turning up the path, he beckoned Don to follow.

Soon they came to a small clearing within a circle of very small, rounded, leaf-covered huts. Smoke rose from several fires inside and in front of the houses. Chickens scratched indifferently in the nearby bushes. No one else was in sight.

The chief invited them inside his little two-room house, each room taking up about six square feet. The ridge pole rose to a height of about four feet and a fire smoldered in the center of the dirt floor of what seemed to be the living room. A few animal skins hung from the walls, but there did not appear to be any fetish altars or idols in the village.

The guide called out to the people he knew were hiding in the forest around them. "It's your ancestor, your uncle from downriver who has come back to be with his own people," he said. "He has come to meet you and to speak with you."

There was only silence. A hornbill suddenly called from the top of a tree. Don cupped his hands around his mouth and perfectly imitated the bird's call. As if on cue, the bird flew down to a branch directly over Don's head. Moments later, about fifteen Pygmies emerged from the bushes, surrounded Don and began to dance around him.

Joe Nicholson, who had been gradually inching toward the village, joined the group. Soon twenty more Pygmies appeared out of the forest, most of them completely naked.

The Pygmies were lighter skinned than the larger tribespeople. Most of the women had large holes in their earlobes and their hair, which was short, showed few signs of braiding or care. The hair of the men and boys, on the other hand, showed evidence of shaving or trimming. Both sexes wore bright strings of beads and either nothing else or tiny, raphia loincloths as their only clothing.

Don, through the interpreter, explained that he and Nicholson had come from a far country across the "great river that has no banks" to tell them about the Great Spirit who made the forest. He and Joe had to continue on their jour-

ney, he told them, but he would come back
again to tell them more about the Great Spirit.
There followed an enthusiastic Pygmy-style,
thumb-shaking farewell. When they had shaken
every thumb in sight several times, the missionaries left the clearing and started back to the
main trail. A parade of chanting Pygmies followed behind. That day the men hiked twenty
miles, arriving finally at the village of Chief
Mabula, the overseer of all that territory.
Mabula was an unusual-looking man with locks
of hair braided down over his forehead, between his eyes and on down into a spindly little
beard that continued almost to his knees. He
had twelve wives who braided his hair and
groomed him almost continuously while he sat
on his chieftain's stool and talked to the two
Americans about his people and his country.

That night, several bearded Pygmy chiefs appeared. They had obviously been running for a
long time, for their bodies were shining with
perspiration and their chests were heaving.

"They want you to go and live with them,"
Jacques told Don, "and to come back to their
village with them tonight." Their next statement took Don's breath away. "They are giving
you the authority to decide for their people
matters of life, death and marriage. They want
you to live with them and to teach them about
the Great Spirit of the forest and the soul of
man." For a moment both missionaries were
speechless. One of the Pygmy chiefs un-

wrapped a beautifully carved stone pipe that had never been smoked and handed it to Don.

"This is an initiation into their tribe," Jacques explained. "You have been taken into this Pygmy clan." Don accepted the pipe with obvious pleasure.

"They expect you to go back with them now," Jacques continued, showing his amusement at Don's predicament. But Don had already been thinking of an answer.

"Tell the chiefs that I have a woman and two children. I cannot remain here and live with them until I go back down the great river that has no far bank, find my woman and children and bring them back with me." Jacques translated and the Pygmy chiefs shook their heads in agreement.

"Isn't that so? Isn't that so?" they murmured to each other. "A man without his woman is helpless. You must go out on the river and find your woman and children and bring them back," they replied. "Your heart will not settle down inside your stomach until you have your woman. Isn't that so?" Everyone, including the oddly braided Chief Mabula, nodded and agreed that it was so.

"How long will it be before you come back with your woman? One moon? Two moons?" they persisted.

"We will come back again," Don explained, knowing they would not be happy with a more specific answer. "The Great Spirit who brought us together today will bring my wife, my children and me back to you. But it will be twelve moons at least." The Pygmy chiefs were disappointed. They talked long into the night with the missionaries.

The next day the missionary party arrived at Chief Kumiki's village of Koto high in the mountains near Mbigou. Once everyone was seated and the missionaries had recounted the news of their travels, the chief responded.

"We know," he said, pointing his walking stick at Don, "that you are the spirit of a great hunter from our country who died and who has come back to his people. We want you to come and live among our people. We want to learn about the Great Spirit that sent you back to us. We will give you land and we will even build you houses if you will live here." It was the most generous and gracious offer the group had received.

Chief Kumiki handled his ebony walking stick like a scepter. It was intricately carved, with bands of brass, copper and iron around it at different levels. Don was fascinated by the stick and asked the chief about it. The chief recounted the history of his ancestors, beginning at the carvings on the lowest level of the stick.

"Now I am here," he said, pointing near the top, "and there is no more room on the stick. I do not know if my family will continue to rule after me. But where my hand rests, that is where I am." Don waited until the chief finished speaking and then made an audacious request.

"Great Chief," he began, "we are returning to Mouila and soon we will return to our country down the great river and beyond the river that has no shores. If we are to return to your country, our own people will have to give us their wealth. How will they know that I have really met you and that you have invited us to return? What will convince them that I am telling the truth about your invitation? May I not take this walking stick to prove to my countrymen that I tell the truth?"

Chief Kumiki and the other chiefs were dumbfounded. The village elders murmured among themselves, shaking their heads in disapproval while Chief Kumiki fingered the carvings. The discussion took a long time, but finally the headshaking stopped.

Chief Kumiki stood to his feet. The missionaries followed suit. Cradling the precious stick in both his hands as though it were glass, the chief presented it to Don.

"I am told by my people that you have treated everyone with respect and kindness. You have taken nothing from our people and have given greater gifts than you have received. You have spoken everywhere of the Great Spirit that sent you to our country and we know that your spirit once lived in our land. We want you to come back and live among your people. You must take the stick back to your land and tell your people that through this stick Chief Kumiki speaks. Tell them that Chief Kumiki's stick is calling for you to return."

Bowing, Don thanked all of the chiefs and the elders. The wily chiefs had turned his simple request for the walking stick into an almost sacred promise to return. As he held the symbol of the chief's authority in his hands, Don realized that if for some reason he did not return with the stick, Kumiki and his people would forever feel betrayed.

On March 30, the thirtieth day of their journey, the party marched through an extremely rich and dense rain forest, alternately drenched by driving storms and steamed by humid heat. Biting flies, including the dreaded tsetse fly, pursued them relentlessly. The jungle creatures grew silent at the strange sound of more than thirty pairs of shuffling feet and thirty pairs of slapping hands.

In the distance the men could hear the soft sounds of a waterfall. The sounds grew louder as the miles passed, until they arrived at a small village of about twenty houses called Makombo. The visitors gratefully settled into a bark-walled, two-room house provided by the chief, a man named Boudiongo.

Fairley and Nicholson were intensely curious about the waterfall. Chief Boudiongo ex-

plained that the river was called the Louétsi
and agreed to guide them the short distance to
the falls. A winding path snaked through the
forest for about a quarter-mile before the
group suddenly emerged at the foot of a thun-
derous waterfall more than eighty feet wide.
Below the falls the river boiled against the
roots of towering hardwood trees and doubled
in width for a quarter of a mile before quieting
and depositing banks of clean sand on the far
shore. A mist ascended from the foot of the
falls into the air and frosted onto the luxuriant
foliage on each side.

For several moments the men stood transfixed by the power and the beauty of the scene
before them. Don asked Chief Boudiongo if he
would take them across the river. He agreed.
Finally safe on the other side after a shaky ride
in tiny canoes, Boudiongo took Don and the
others up the steep bank to several hills that
rose sharply from the river. There seemed to be
three hills, the highest starting a half-mile
above the falls, the next beginning just below
the falls and the third another 500 yards downriver. Between the highest and second hill a ravine led to the river. The second and third hills
were separated by a small stream that emptied
into the widest part of the river close to where
their canoes had landed. The highest hill fell
away in a steep 300-foot drop to the river
above the falls, exposing rugged cliffs of gray
limestone. From the size and density of the

great trees, it was obvious to Don that for more than fifty years no one had cleared the land on any of the three hills either for gardens or for houses. "Why?" he wondered aloud.

The chief hesitated for a moment, then led the group on a small trail to a precipitous clearing overlooking the falls. At the very bottom of the clearing a four-foot wide limestone rock jutted out into space, looming fifty feet over the frenzied white water below. The group paused in the clearing, staying well away from the edge.

"This is the place where people who have been convicted of eating the souls of others are thrown into the river to die," Boudiongo began nervously. "If you listen carefully, you can hear in the roar of the water the cries of the spirits of those who died. That is why no one lives here or makes his plantation here. It is a sacred place, a place of death." Though Don had a dozen questions to ask, Boudiongo abruptly turned and led the group away without further comment. *How important is that rock to him?* Don wondered as he followed silently.

Of all the sites they had seen, this was by far the most promising. The soil in the ravine and along the stream was rich and excellent for gardening, and up on the hills the clay was suitable for making bricks. To be certain that the stone could be used to make lime cement, Don put a piece of the rock in his pocket to take back to the States to be assayed. *Perhaps,* he thought to himself, *we could even build a hydro-electric plant!*

His report to Joe Nicholson, who had not crossed the river, was just slightly less than ecstatic. That night as they sat around the campfire in Makombo, Chief Boudiongo told the visitors that the waterfalls were called Bongolo, but he did not know why. He told them that the river was full of large fish, that there were no crocodiles until several miles below the falls, that herds of game lived and foraged for food on the opposite side of the river and that the river was navigable all the way to Mouila. He listed nearly forty villages within one day's walk of Makombo and told the missionaries that while the Banzebi people were the predominant tribe, 120 villages of Bapounou, Mitsogo, Massangou and Bavoumbou lay within half a day's walk.

That night, as they had done throughout their trip, the missionaries recounted the story of Christ. Chief Boudiongo made no response to their invitation, but when they had finished talking he pleaded with them to live among his people and establish their mission on the land across the river. It almost seemed as though he was anxious to end his control over the dreaded execution rock of Bongolo.

On April 13, 1933, the steamer with Nicholson and Fairley pulled away from the dock at Mouila and headed downriver to take them back to Lambaréné. Their journey had lasted fifty-five days and had covered over 1,000 kilometers (665 miles).

When Don learned that the Mission board wanted him and Dorothy to return as soon as possible to the States to raise funds before returning to work in South Gabon, he took the next steamboat home. On May 11, 1933, he was reunited with Dorothy, Bonnie Jeanne and Gordon. He had been gone for three months.

7

Engaging the Enemy

"But my righteous one will live by faith. And if he shrinks back, I will not be pleased with him." Hebrews 10:38

The United States was in the fourth year of the Great Depression in 1933 when Don, then 28, and Dorothy, 26, returned for their first furlough. Many people in Alliance churches were out of work or experiencing other financial hardship. The Mission board had cut missionary allowances by forty percent and churches were struggling to support the missionaries that were already in place. Nevertheless, the Alliance leaders were keenly interested in Don's report about South Gabon.

After discussing it, the board decided to go forward. But they insisted on one important condition: Before any missionaries could enter South Gabon, the Fairleys would have to raise

$5,000. The money would pay for transportation, for the cost of building a mission station and for their allowances for the first several years.

During the Great Depression $5,000 was a small fortune. Undaunted, the Fairleys returned to Santa Barbara brimming with optimism. After all, what was $5,000 to the Creator of the universe? Did He not own the cattle on a thousand hills? They spoke in churches from Chicago to Nebraska, Iowa, Wisconsin, Colorado and Southern California recounting the story of Chief Kumiki's walking stick and holding it up before people as proof that they spoke as the chief's representative.

Several months after his adventure in the south, Ndoba wrote to Jean Mbadinga. He gave no details about his trip, stating simply that two American missionaries had come to Lambaréné, had traveled in the south and had promised to return the following year to establish a Protestant mission. Mbadinga was ecstatic.

Several months later he finished his studies and was assigned to teach at the French Protestant School in Port Gentil. On his way there he stopped at Lambaréné and quizzed Ndoba about his trip. The director of the Mission gave Mbadinga Don Fairley's address in the United States. He immediately wrote Don telling him who he was and asking him to take him with him when he returned to South Gabon. When Don received the letter several months later, any lingering doubts about his mission vanished forever.

Despite the Fairley's fund-raising zeal, their efforts produced little excitement. They looked distressingly younger than their twenty-some years, they had spent a mere two years in Africa and, next to the great missionaries of that era, they were virtually unknown. By the end of twelve months only $200 had come in for the project. What did it mean? Had they somehow misunderstood God? The answer seemed obvious to everyone but Dr. Snead. Hoping and praying for a miracle, he encouraged the Fairleys to continue their efforts and extended their furlough an additional two months.

The burden for Gabon also fell heavily on the heart of the treasurer of The Christian and Missionary Alliance, William Christie, a man known for his years of service as a pioneer missionary in Northeast Tibet and China. In each church where the Fairleys preached, Dr. Christie followed and presented again the urgent need to enter Gabon. In church after church he pled with the people to pray that at the end of the two-month extension God would supply all that was needed. Little by little, money began to come in for the project. With just a few weeks remaining, a total of $1,000 had been collected. Combined with the money raised by

the missionaries and the national Church in
the Belgian Congo, the total came to $2,000.

Only two weeks remained on the Fairleys'
furlough extension when Don went to the Gospel Tabernacle in Omaha, Nebraska. The pastor of the church was Dr. R.R. Brown.
Weighing in at around 100 pounds and, looking inexperienced and unimpressive, Don
showed his pictures and spoke from his heart.
Holding Chief Kumiki's stick before the congregation, he appealed one last time for the
people of South Gabon. As he finished his
message, Dr. Christie arrived at the back of the
church, having just come from the train station. He walked directly to the front of the
church and climbed onto the platform. The old
missionary preached with such passion that
many in the congregation began to weep.

When he finished, Dr. Brown announced
that a special offering would be taken for Gabon. As the plates were passed, many removed
rings and watches and dropped them in. When
everything was counted, the total came to
more than $3,000. The congregation erupted
in joy. Dr. Christie turned to Don.

"Young man, go back and get Dorothy and
your children and bring them to New York.
You are at last on your way!"

The day after the final meeting in Omaha,
Don left for Santa Barbara where he and
Dorothy began packing. He stopped long
enough to take Chief Kumiki's walking stick to

a jeweler. Guided by Don's instructions, the jeweler added to the top of the stick a gleaming, one-inch-wide band of silver engraved in French: "For God so loved the world that he gave his one and only Son, that whoever believes in him shall not perish but have eternal life."

Don also had the piece of white rock he had picked up at the Bongolo Falls assayed by a geologist. It turned out to be a high grade limestone, ideal for making lime and lime cement.

By the time the Fairleys arrived in Gabon, a total of $8,000 had come in for the project. Given at great personal sacrifice by God's people during the fourth year of the Great Depression, the money covered all of the expenses and construction during the first four years of the project, enabling the missionaries to at last unlock the doors of Bwiti's and Mwiri's prison-kingdom.

Early on December 20, 1934, the second morning after the Fairleys' arrival in Port Gentil, a young Gabonese showed up outside their guest house door.

"Monsieur Fayley! Monsieur Fayley! Allo! A-lloo-oh!"

Don leaned out the upstairs window and stared in surprise at the well-dressed young man standing below.

"What do you want?" he asked, trying to dispel the sleep and irritation from his voice.

"I want to talk with you! I am Jean Mbadinga! I wrote you a letter in America!" As the
words began to jog Don's memory, he smiled
and nodded in acknowledgment.

"Just a minute, I'll be down!" he responded.

After shaking hands and briefly sizing each
other up, Don and Mbadinga sat down.

"Do you work as a pastor here?" Don asked,
trying to remember what Jean had written in
his letter.

"No, I teach in the Protestant school in Lambaréné," Mbadinga replied. "The pastor of our
church told me that you had come." For several minutes they talked about Port Gentil, the
weather and Mbadinga's job before he came to
the point.

"I want to go with you into the south,"
Mbadinga finally said. "I am Bapounou and I
want my people to know about Jesus. I want to
work for you." Mbadinga's directness surprised
Don.

"What will your superiors say? Do they know
about this?" Don asked.

"I don't know what they will say. I have asked
to go with you before, but they said they need
me too much. If you want me to come with
you, you will have to ask them." For almost an
hour the two men talked, each probing the
other, each liking what he found.

Finally Don said, "When I get to Lambaréné,
I will ask your superiors about you. If they give
me a good report and if the other missionary

who is coming is in agreement, we will ask them to let you go with us."

The next day the Fairleys loaded their trunks and crates onto a paddle wheel steamboat and boarded. Around noon the boat began the thirty-hour trip upriver. They arrived at the Protestant Mission of Ngomo on Christmas day, 1934.

Meanwhile, in the Belgian Congo, the Alliance missionaries voted to send their chairman, Harold Pierson, his wife Ozzie and their seven-year-old son LeRoy to Gabon to oversee the establishment of the new work. The Fairleys had spent only two years in Africa and it did not seem likely that they would succeed if left on their own. The Piersons and Fairleys were supposed to arrive simultaneously, but after waiting a week at the French Mission at Andendé across from Lambaréné, Don became impatient.

While they waited, Faustin Ndoba came to see Don. He seemed discouraged and forlorn, though he didn't say why. Despite his promise to follow Jesus Christ in baptism after his near-drowning, he still had not been baptized. When Don said that he was looking for a cook to accompany them south, Ndoba said he needed time to consult his family before answering. The next day he returned saying he would come.

There could hardly have been two more different people in the world than Harold Pierson and Don Fairley. Harold was a tall, balding, slow-moving, reflective, patient and methodical man. He had a strong belief that God was leading their Mission into the south, but he also believed that poor planning would result in failure. If and when decisions had to be made, he would not, indeed could not, be rushed. His answers were long in coming and reflected an innate caution. Fluent in Kikongo, he spoke French with some difficulty.

Like Harold, Don held an unshakable belief that if God was with them, no problem was insurmountable. But there the similarities ended. Don bordered on short, had plenty of hair and moved like a nervous gazelle. He was fluent in French and learned the tribal languages with ease, often speaking as the Africans did in animal-life parables. He also overflowed with energy, optimism, enthusiasm and untried ideas. Innately adventurous, he believed that the failure to try was the worst failure of all. He seemed to believe that God could overcome any blunder as long as it sprang from a rightly motivated idea. Don was so accustomed to looking at the bright side of disaster that discouragement slid off of him like water off a duck's back. He had a quick and ready answer to any question and tended to be impatient. Could God, would God use such a team to invade the kingdom of Mwiri and Bwiti?

The American missionaries requested the Evangelical Paris Mission that Jean Mbadinga

and Marc Divingou, who had been trained as a
carpenter at the Ngomo Mission, be allowed to
join them in the south. The request for Jean
Mbadinga met with heated opposition and
lengthy discussion. But the Americans argued
convincingly that God had surely called and
prepared Mbadinga to return with the gospel
to his own people. Since the Alliance was going
to the Bapounous, it was only logical that
Mbadinga work with them.

The French missionaries reluctantly agreed
to let Mbadinga go after they had found someone to replace him. They also agreed to let
Marc Divingou go with them. Like Mbadinga
and Ndoba, Marc Divingou had left his village
as a boy to go north to Lambaréné. There he
became a Christian, attended the school and
learned carpentry. To the credit of the French
missionaries, they not only gave up two of their
best helpers, they also prayed and asked God
to bless the Alliance expedition. Perhaps they
knew how easily it could end in disaster.

In the weeks before setting out, the Piersons
and the Fairleys discussed strategy in some detail. The first thing they had to do was not to
preach, but to befriend. They would do that by
living as families among the people and learning to speak their languages. The French government would only give them land if they built
permanent houses of either hardwood or brick
on land they officially requested. After much
prayer, they agreed upon the following strat-

egy: (1) The two men would choose a site for a permanent Mission and hire workers to clear the land and build a temporary house out of materials from the rain forest. As soon as a house was built, one of the men would return to Lambaréné to bring the wives and children to the new station. (2) They would clear and plant gardens large enough to support them and their paid helpers. (3) They would begin preaching the gospel to the hired workmen from the very beginning. Their Bible teaching would be systematic, beginning with the creation story and ending with the return of Jesus Christ. (4) They would baptize only those believers who made a clear break from the past by burning their fetishes and seeking to live godly lives. (5) They would establish a church at the first mission center, train both men and women evangelists from among the believers to return to their own villages with the gospel and establish additional mission centers and churches as God permitted until all of the southern tribes had heard the gospel. (6) They would not insist on Western church and worship forms, but would establish an African church, led by Africans, whose goal would be to become self-supporting.

Harold Pierson finished selecting the members of the expedition, collected and cataloged the supplies, pored over maps and questioned Don in detail about the various locations he and Joe Nicholson had studied. At last he felt prepared. The initial party would consist of Harold, Don, Faustin Ndoba, a Bapounou named Mapaga and the carpenter Marc Divingou.

On February 25, 1935, the five men loaded six doors, ten windows, cots, mosquito nets, tins of fuel, a crate of machetes, axes, hoes, shovels, boxes of canned foods, rifles and ammunition onto a commercial steamboat headed for Sindara. As the wives and children waved from the steps of the little chapel on the shore, the men rowed the newly built, twenty-foot launch out into deeper water. Don gave several violent pulls on the outboard motor before the first piston fired, emitting a cloud of blue smoke. A moment later the second piston caught with a roar and Don dropped the spinning propeller into the water. Minutes later the boat was little more than a smudge on the great river.

Several days and villages later, the expedition reached the Louétsi River and five kilometers later their ears picked up the roar of Bongolo Falls. Chief Boudiongo met them at the village entrance. He threw back his head and, laughing with delight, pumped Don's hand vigorously. Don presented Harold and the rest of their party to Chief Boudiongo and through a translator explained that they had come to look over the area.

Late that afternoon Boudiongo took the missionaries across the river below the falls in the tiny canoes Don remembered so well. From every vantage point, the chief extended his arm and pointed out the lands in the distance where lived the Massangou, the Mitsogo, the Bapounou, the Bavoumbou and his own people, the Banzebi. At Don's request, he again showed them the white execution rock overhanging the river above the falls.

Harold Pierson tramped back and forth until it seemed he had trod over every square inch of the hills both above and below the falls. By now, Don knew Harold well enough to see that he was impressed with the site he favored.

When they returned to the village that afternoon they found it filled with visitors who had come to see the strangers. That night, for the first time, the missionaries told the crowd the story of Jesus. At the end of their talk, Chief Boudiongo stood, placed a hand over his heart and said, "My heart will never again rest nor my sleep be peaceful until you have built your house next to mine." It was a moving gesture, but they did not know the chief well enough to judge his sincerity. They would soon find out just how sincere he was.

The missionaries and their three helpers remained in the village of Makombo for nearly a week, sleeping in the single-room, bark house Chief Boudiongo had provided for them and eating his food.

Several days later, twelve angry-looking men filed into Makombo led by two who were dressed like Europeans. They were religious teachers from the new Catholic Mission between Mbigou and Bongolo. Each of the men carried the walking stick of one the chiefs of the surrounding villages, indicating that he had been authorized to speak for the chief whose stick he held.

In the year since Don and Joe Nicholson had made their trip, a Catholic priest had established a mission in Chief Kumiki's territory. During the previous two days the group had visited more than twenty villages, explaining that the white men who had arrived in Makombo were evil strangers falsely masquerading as priests who had come to poison the people and eat the souls of their children. The village chiefs were so alarmed that they agreed to immediately drive the strangers out of their territory.

The visitors ordered Harold and Don to leave Makombo immediately. They then turned to Chief Boudiongo, ordered him to give the strangers no further assistance or food and demanded that he drive them out of his village by the next day. Chief Boudiongo listened politely, but said nothing.

The visitors remained all day, arguing and talking with the people, threatening violence if they were not obeyed and leaving behind them a cloud of fear. When the missionaries got up the next morning, the usual hustle and bustle of the village had been replaced by a strange silence. Most of the people of Makombo had slipped away to their plantations. There was nothing to do but pray for God to help them.

Chief Boudiongo acted as though nothing had happened. During the next few days he and Chief Boukangou, who was responsible for land distribution in the area, took the visitors through all the territory for miles around. To the north, within half a day's march, they found large and numerous villages of both the Mitsogo and Massangou people.

The missionaries were fast running out of food and Boudiongo's gardens could not feed them indefinitely. That evening they invited the people to another meeting. Only about half the village attended and listened as they talked about the Creator-God, the first man and woman, Satan's deception and the fall of man and woman under the power of sin. None but Boudiongo declared themselves willing to follow the God of the white strangers.

On Tuesday, March 19, Harold decided they needed a morning to fast, meditate and pray to hear the still, small voice of God. Harold, Don, Mapaga, Ndoba, Divingou and Chief Boukangou crossed the river and once again climbed to the hills above Bongolo Falls. For a while they stood on execution rock. They sensed nothing sinister about the place. Although wild and beautiful, it was also restful. The two missionaries climbed back up the hill and sat down under separate trees to meditate and pray.

Around noon Harold stood and walked over to where Don sat slumped against a tree.

"I think this is where God wants us to build," he said simply. Don stood and stretched, a smile of relief on his face. Harold Pierson was the senior missionary and the man in charge. Such a decision could not be made without his complete approval.

"We think this is where God wants us to build," Harold explained to the group, gesturing in a wide circle around him.

Back in Makombo, Chief Boudiongo greeted the missionaries' decision with a shout loud enough to bring people out of their houses. But only a few men could be found to help with the clearing. As they were wondering what to do next, the answer appeared with almost comic pomp and fanfare.

Into the sleepy village strode a garishly dressed "soldier" accompanied by a small entourage, including his wife and several attendants. Approaching the astonished missionaries and their host, he snapped to attention, slapped the butt of his gun to the ground, saluted, then smiled. A black hole appeared between his lips where all of his upper and lower front teeth were missing. While the missionaries struggled to hide their amusement, the villagers were profoundly impressed. The missionaries soon discovered that

the Africans' perception of the soldier was closer
to the truth than their own.

Opening the leather pouch hanging from
his shoulder, the soldier presented Harold
with a letter from the French administrator at
Mbigou, fifty miles away. The letter welcomed the missionaries to the Mbigou district and authorized them to move into the
government guest house in Makombo and
stay in it as long as they wished! The French
commander went on to say that he had ordered his soldier to make certain that the
people in the area provided them with all the
food they required. Furthermore, he had
commissioned his man to conscript people
from all of the nearby villages to clear the forest, build and make gardens and clear wide
paths to the new mission site. The administrator informed them that within five days he
would come in person to meet them and to
see that all was well. He ended his letter by
saying that his representative was authorized
to "do whatever you deem necessary to arrive
at the accomplishment of your mission."

As the missionaries looked up from the letter,
the soldier explained that he had already ordered the territorial chief and all of the district
chiefs to come to Makombo for a meeting.
Furthermore, on his way from Mbigou he had
passed through many villages and had ordered
the chiefs to send people to Makombo to help
the Americans.

The previously quiet village soon exploded with activity. Under the soldier's stern direction, the new conscripts repaired the government guest house and rebuilt its outbuildings. They made a wide path from the river up to the Mission building site and cleared a landing on the river's edge. As the missionaries worked alongside the conscripts, the people gradually lost their fear. Soon they began to laugh and joke as they passed on the paths.

That evening the missionaries met with a sullen group of chiefs gathered from the Banzebi, Bapounou, Mitsogo and Massangou villages in the area. The missionaries explained who they were, why they had come and how they hoped to help the people. Their gentleness and courtesy contrasted sharply with the authoritarian manner of other whites in the area. By the end of the meeting, the chiefs' fear and mistrust had begun to melt. Together they laid plans to gather building materials from the forest for the houses the missionaries needed to build.

In the week that followed, more than fifty men passed through Makombo carrying their annual tax of palm nuts to Mouila. Most of them asked if on their return from Mouila they could be hired as porters to carry back from Mouila the rest of the missionaries' supplies. Don signed up fifty of them and the next morning left for Mouila in the launch.

Meanwhile, Harold supervised a crew of 107 men and women who cleared the underbrush, felled the huge trees with axes and handsaws and chopped them into lengths that could later be cut into boards. Most of the trees on the hill turned out to be hardwood and were so huge that it took several days to chop and saw through them. When they fell, the earth trembled.

The enormous task of clearing the land was well underway when Don returned. Among the supplies the porters carried was a case of 100 urgently needed machetes. But when Harold and Don opened the case they discovered that the machetes had not been sharpened at the factory. What were they to do?

Chief Boudiongo learned of their dilemma and sent for a man from a nearby village who made knives. A few days later Nzengue appeared. Don was surprised to learn that Nzengue spoke French as well as the languages of both the Bapounous and the Banzebis. When Don showed him the machetes, he immediately set to work heating the blades and hammering the edges sharp. By the end of one week he had sharpened all 100 machetes. Don asked him to stay.

The missionaries decided to hold a service every morning after the people had eaten. The workers liked the idea and gathered in the shade to hear how the world began, how evil came into the world and how God had allowed His Son to be killed to conquer evil. It was the

Donald and Dorothy Fairley on their wedding day, September 1, 1926 in Santa Barbara, California. They were 21 and 19 years old respectively.

Back row L to R: Bonnie, Gordon;
Front row L to R: Peggy, Don, Dottie, Dorothy, Betty Anne, 1946.

Dorothy wrote, "We sent our two young children, Bonnie Jeanne and Gordon, ages 8 and 6 years, home to America . . . where they continued their education in private Christian boarding schools . . . . Our family was united only on our furloughs every fifth year." This shows a happy 1939 reunion.

Chief Mboudi, the chief of all the Bavoumbou and one of the first to follow the Jesus Way.

Dépinga Daniel, chief of the Bongolo Pygmy clan.

Pygmy Christians ready for the hunt.

Chief Boudiongo (circa 1935) encouraged Pierson and Fairley to establish their mission at the Bongolo site. Two of his sons eventually became pastors of some of the largest churches in Gabon.

Dorothy's special friend—a pygmy woman with her grandchild.

The first house at Bongolo, circa 1934, surrounded by literacy students and student evangelists.

Bongolo's first open-sided meeting house could seat a packed crowd of 200. Dorothy is at the organ, Don and children nearby; 1935.

The Bavoumbou turn to Christ (note skulls). Waldo Schindler, second from left.

L to R: Paul Ndoba, unknown, Joseph Nicholson, Don Fairley, unknown, ready for initial 1933 survey trip.

A Pygmy couple.

Lebongo Etienne, the first Bavoumbou believer, burns his fetishes.
Hundreds followed his example.

An early baptism in the Louétsi River, 1936.

Don and young friends, 1941.

A group of porters listen to a gospel preesentation. (Note the size of their baskets, also the banana leaves on the ground where others have been sitting.)

An early literacy class with Jean Mbadinga at Bongolo.
The language was not yet written.

Bongolo's first dispensary, circa 1944.

Students in the 1940s were taught the Word of God plus reading and writing.

Don Fairley—husband, father, preacher, teacher, hunter, builder, electrician, carpenter, gardener, animal trainer, welder, handyman par excellence. One missionary colleague noted: "Sometimes it seemed like he knew how to do almost everything." The Pygmies called him "Tata Ngu na Ngu"—"Mr. Here and There."

The completed hydro-electric plant, 1945. Workmen removed more than 20 tons of rock from the site, rafted heavy machinery and dragged it 90 feet to the worksite.

The Fairley's Renault was the first missionary car on the field; 1943.

School buildings and worker's house where the Bongolo hospital now stands.

Because of shooting this elephant and sharing the meat, Don was able to gain access to a formerly hostile Pygmy group.

The Gabon missionary family circa 1941. L to R: Raymond Cook with baby Earlyne, Helen Cook, Don Fairley, Dorothy Fairley, Cecil Schindler, Furman Lentz (behind), Waldo Schindler.
Front row L to R: Rae Joyce Cook, Margaret Fairley, Lois Schindler.

Betty Anne Fairley with Dr. Albert Schweitzer who delivered her. Pictures were taken only with his permission— no candid shots allowed.

Marc Divingou, third from right, with saw, and the carpenters he trained and discipled. In 1956, he was elected as the first church president. Today his son is the director of numerous Christian schools operated by the Alliance Church of Gabon.

Harold Pierson with Pygmy friend.

Dorothy teaching village women.

Pastor Paul Ndoba and Lois, 1993. Although named "Deception" and abused by his family, Paul became a key to reaching his tribe, the Eshira. He also served as the third president of the Gabon Christian Alliance Church (1969-1974).

John Mboudi, 1994 (left). John worked at the Bongolo dispensary and eventually became a consular official at the Gabonese embassy in Washington D.C. and Gabon's representative to the United Nations.

Jean Mbadinga, 1994. His school at Bongolo was the first of its kind in the south, drawing students from various competing tribes. Many of them became pastors and church leaders. John was the second church president.

Right: Don poses with a Pygmy chief who refused to "ride in the belly of an elephant (car)." Don's barely 5'9" frame stands in sharp contrast to the height of the chief.

Center: Don and Paul Ndoba baptize believers at Bongolo.

Bottom: The interior of the Bongalo church which Don built in 1955. Exterior view, next page.

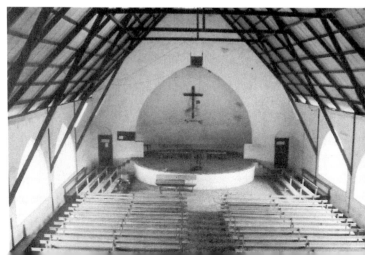

Left: Don and Dorothy pose with Pastor Paul Ndoba two years before their retirement from active missionary service in 1969.

Center: The Bongolo Church, 1955.

Bottom: The Bongolo ferry as seen in the 1950s. As of 1994, a 240-foot concrete and steel bridge spans the Louétsi River and provides unrestricted access to the Bongolo hospital.

A 1940s missionary display features a fetish drum "deserted by Pygmy Christian community" and other pictures and paraphenalia. A story related by Don's son Gordon, tells how after speaking harshly to a Pygmy visiting from a distant village, Don later walked two weeks to apologize to the man. Such was Don's love for God—and for the Pygmies.

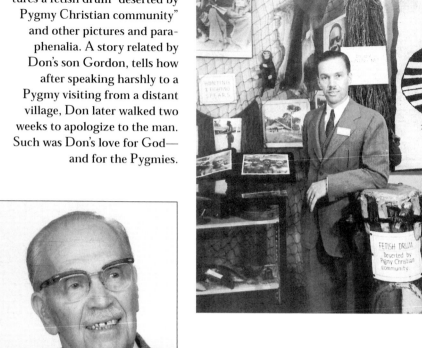

This photo celebrates Don's 80th birthday, 1986. Dorothy preceded him to heaven in 1982. Don was reunited with her 1990.

The Gabonese government decorated Don "in recognition of services rendered to the people of the Gabon Republic," June 1964.

This portrait celebrated Donald and Dorothy's 50th wedding anniversary, September 1, 1966.

strangest story they had ever heard, but they could not stop listening. After a restful hour of singing and listening to Bible teaching, they seemed content to return to work for a few more hours.

Soon after the missionaries started this practice, Chief Boudiongo asked them to hold similar meetings six nights a week in his village. By this time the chief had wholeheartedly accepted the gospel message and had many questions, including what to do about his six wives.

After only two weeks the people had cleared and leveled an area large enough for work to begin on the main house. By this time many of the workers had to return home to tend to their own gardens and to their children. The favorable reports that the first helpers took back to their villages produced immediate replacements. The word quickly spread that the two white men who had come were already beginning to speak their languages and that, unlike the colonialists, they worked alongside the people and spoke gently to them. Hundreds of people appeared out of the forest from every direction, curious to see the white strangers for themselves and willing to help in exchange for rock salt or a machete.

Since the missionaries had been unable to bring either hammers or nails, Harold made plans to build a single large mud-wattle house. In mid-April he and Don marked out the site.

The house would be forty feet long, twenty feet wide, with a large living room, a dining room, two bedrooms, a shower room, a kitchen and a storeroom.

Within a week Harold had erected upright hardwood posts every two feet to form the inside and outside walls. He linked these posts together every four inches with horizontal strips of split palm branches, tying the palm branches to the posts with small vines. Don sent fifty men to Ivouta to pick up the palm shingles they had ordered and other teams of men into the forest to search for vines and palm branches. Two days later the men returned from Ivouta empty-handed—the Catholic teacher had persuaded the people not to help them.

When the wall frames were up and the roofing poles were tied in place, Harold was ready to have the people apply the mud. They had never seen a house built this way and were fascinated by Harold's design. The house was going up so rapidly that Harold decided Don should go after their wives and children in the launch. It had been two months since they had separated.

The news at Andendé was not good. A week after Harold and Don left for Bongolo, the Pierson's seven-year old son and only child, LeRoy, began to cough. As the days passed into weeks, LeRoy's cough worsened and he began to run a constant, low-grade fever. Mrs. Pierson finally took him to see Dr. Schweitzer. He concluded that LeRoy was suffering from tuberculosis and advised Ozzie to take the boy back to the United States for treatment as soon as possible.

When Don arrived in Lambaréné after a four-day trip, his joy in seeing Dorothy and the children was quickly dampened by the news of LeRoy's illness. For two months Ozzie Pierson had sewed curtains and mended clothes in a damp and leaky house. She wanted in the worst way to go with LeRoy to Bongolo to at least see the site. But Don convinced her that the trip would be dangerous for the boy and would only complicate the work. She would have to wait alone in Lambaréné until Harold could come.

Don sent a letter from Dr. Schweitzer to Harold by runner. Letter in hand, Harold hired a canoe and immediately headed for Lambaréné. A few days later, Harold turned over his official correspondence, accounts and remaining funds to Don. And within two weeks the Piersons were on a steamer headed for the United States.

After saying goodbye to the Pierson family, the Fairleys loaded up the launch and, praying for God's protection, headed upriver. After three hours of increasingly swift currents, they

approached Digaba Falls. The falls were only
forty feet high, but they were 300 yards wide.
After some men at Digaba helped them carry
the launch around the falls, Don hired a guide
and they carefully worked their way upriver,
creeping around boulders, looking for eddies
and whirlpools and studying the current. It
took them nearly an hour to climb another 500
yards.

After a respite of calm water they came again
to an area of turbulence. As the launch entered
the churning water the prow swung around to
follow the water downstream toward the falls.
Don turned the outboard to counter the pull of
the whirlpool, but again and again huge caul-
drons of boiling water tipped and spun them,
shooting them downstream toward the falls
without warning. On one of these terrifying
spinouts they slammed into a series of partially
submerged rocks. The cotter pin on the propeller shaft sheared off. The motor screamed out
of control.

The current immediately swept them off the
rocks and flung them once again toward the
falls at a terrifying speed. The launch tipped
and spun through the same whirlpools and currents they had just spent an hour coming
through and, though the men grabbed desper-
ately at rocks and tree trunks lying in the river
along their watery path, they could not hold
on. Dorothy clutched her children and prayed
aloud, her eyes closed in fear. Uppermost in all

of their minds was the knowledge that at the rate they were descending, they would reach the falls in minutes.

After what seemed like an eternity, the launch slammed onto a submerged boulder. Hesitating between the currents and the rocks, it balanced in the middle of the river. The guide leaped from the prow and, standing neck-deep in the water, held the front end so it faced the current head-on. Despite his effort, the boat continued to wobble, threatening to capsize. Dorothy looked to her left and saw a large rock just under the surface. For a moment she forgot her terror and, putting her leg over the side of the launch, stood in the boat and pushed on the rock with all her strength. The launch stabilized.

Don pulled the motor out of the water and removed the broken cotter pin. The children stopped crying and sat white and silent. As Don worked, his hands trembling almost uncontrollably, Dorothy cried out to God in prayer. Don removed the pin and replaced it with a spare. It seemed to take forever.

The launch was tilted so that the prow was down in the water and the stern up in the air. Before the motor could do any good, they would have to push the launch back out into the current and restart the motor. Don was concerned that if he could not restart the motor in time, they would be swept over the falls. There was nothing else to do but try.

When he gave the signal, Dorothy pulled her foot inside the boat and held the children, once again praying aloud for God to come to their rescue. The guide gradually eased his hold and, planting his feet on the rock that held the launch, pushed the prow out into the current. The water seized the launch, dragged it off the rock and spun it hurtling downriver once again. As they slammed into rock after rock Don tried to steady himself enough to pull on the starter rope. Unbelievably, on the first pull the motor roared to life. Don dropped the propeller into the water, made a shaky turn and once again had control of the launch. The river had swept them to within 200 yards of the falls.

Two hours later they made it out of the rapids and into calm water. Don beached the launch at the village of Ivouta and once again talked with the chiefs about making and selling them thatch shingles for their new house in Bongolo. By this time the Catholic teacher had gone, so the chiefs agreed to provide the shingles.

The next morning the Fairleys resumed their journey. Don was confident that with mostly smooth water before them they would arrive at Bongolo by early afternoon. As the launch hummed up the winding river, its passengers gazed in wonder at the beauty of the virgin forest. Troupes of monkeys screamed and chattered in the trees above them, and brilliant blue kingfishers flashed back and forth across the river, catching small fish in their orange beaks. The beauty around them made them temporarily forget the terrors of the day before.

Around noon dark clouds began to gather, and soon the wind touched the tops of the trees. Dorothy and the guide lowered the canvas sides from the launch's roof and tied them down to the sides. Suddenly, a curtain of water roared down upon them. The wind blew as though in competition with the rain, tearing at the canvas until it finally ripped one side free from its attachments and shredded the other. The tarp flapped wildly for a moment, then fell into the water and floated away. They were now completely exposed to the wind and rain.

Soon after, a second storm hit them, then a third. The swift current, strong winds and heavy load consumed so much fuel that Don had to repeatedly shut off the motor to refill the fuel tank. As the afternoon faded and the evening shadows darkened around them, Don drained their last five-gallon can of gas into the tank. For the first time, he realized they might run out of fuel, daylight or both before reaching Bongolo.

When the fourth storm hit, the rain fell out of sky with such force and intensity that the launch began to fill with water. Then hail began to fall. The stinging ice rained down on them and rattled angrily against the bottom and sides of the boat. By now the childrens' lips were blue with cold, and even Don trembled so violently that he considered pulling over to the shore until the storm had passed.

Then, through the sheets of rain, they vaguely perceived a high, tree-covered bank on the right and a widening of the river. The guide began to shout, waving Don to turn into the mouth of an estuary on the left. They had reached Bongolo.

In moments, a crowd of people arrived on the sandy shore. They gazed in astonishment at the blue-lipped, shivering children and the three exhausted adults. The pouring rain precluded formal greetings, so the people reached into the launch and lifted the unresisting children into their arms. Others grabbed the water-logged supplies and half-carried, half-dragged the weary missionaries the half-mile to Makombo. Murmuring in sympathy, the people took them to the chief's house, lay mats on the floor in a circle around a fire in the central room and gave them roasted sweet potatoes. Sitting close to the fire for warmth, the travelers ate a few bites, then lay fully clothed on the mats and, oblivious to the smoke-filled room and the stares of the crowd, fell into an exhausted sleep.

It was 1934.

8

Base Camp

"I will fear no evil, for you are with me."
Psalm 23:4

During the next eighteen months Don and Dorothy Fairley and their small band of helpers worked fourteen-hour days clearing four acres of land on the three adjoining hills. They cut paths, planted nearly an acre of gardens, built several bark and thatch houses and finished the large, mud-wattled house in the center of the clearing. At the beginning, the missionaries found themselves supervising nearly 200 volunteers, but within a month the number of paid workmen stabilized at around sixty.

For the first eighteen months, the Fairleys were virtually the only white people at Bongolo. Dorothy cooked African-style over an open campfire. Bread was baked in a hole dug in the hillside. This "cave," equipped with a door made from a flattened five-gallon kerosene tin and the hot coals inside eventually yielded delicious steam-cooked, soot-flecked bread. Peanuts were pressed to make oil as well as peanut "milk" for orphaned babies. The Fairleys also made their own soap, tanned their own leather and, on rare vacation days, caught and canned or salted fish. The wild meat Don shot—a lifetime total of more than 200 buffalo, one elephant and many wild antelope and hogs—provided meat for themselves, their co-workers, helpers and school children. Don also raised the first domestic cattle in South Gabon solely for meat and managed to keep a flock of chickens despite the hungry snakes, prowling leopards and driver ants that could wipe out the work of months in one night.

He also grafted a variety of fruits on a wild orange trunk—tangelos, grapefruit, lemons, limes, tangerines, mandarin oranges and citrons, among others. The tree eventually became a tourist attraction.

During this time, Don and Dorothy learned just how much the people feared Bwiti and Mwiri and how viciously these two gods controlled their every thought. In response, they chose a simple strategy they had already discussed with the Piersons: to systematically preach the truth of the gospel.

In the midst of the clearing and building, Don led two meetings a day, each lasting from one to two hours. And in the evenings he and Dorothy wrote reports and letters by lantern light. From the first rays of light until they lay down to sleep at night, a continual stream of visitors came to greet them and to see what was going on at the new mission. Bands of Pygmies, village chiefs from the many tribal groups in the south and newcomers all arrived hoping for work. Only the aggressive and warlike Bavoumbou tribal chiefs stayed away, but some of their people came, among them an intelligent young man named Etienne Lebongo. Within a few months he was soundly converted.

One week after the Fairleys arrived in Ma-kombo, Jean Mbadinga joined them, bringing the number of adults in their band to eight. Mbadinga preached in some of the morning and evening meetings. The people were astonished that an African understood so much about the white man's God.

The main house took far longer to complete than anyone had anticipated. Once the thatch was in place, the walls were mudded, but the ten-foot high walls dried so slowly that for nearly a month the workers kept fires burning continuously inside the rooms. The floors were covered with "jungle cement"—crushed termite mounds mixed with water, smoothed one to two inches thick and pounded with the heavy end of palm branches as it dried. The result was a durable, smooth, easy-to-sweep floor throughout the seven rooms.

When the mud walls had at last dried, the workmen smeared a special white clay from a nearby stream on them, giving the house an attractive whitewashed appearance. The entire structure was built without a single nail and, with the exception of the doors and windows, was built out of materials from the forest. To the Africans, it was a palace.

While Don worked to complete the house and clear the land for gardens, Dorothy translated hymns and portions of the Gospel of Mark. She also treated the village children, using her small supply of aspirin and quinine. When the children recovered, the women came to her for advice on other matters. Eventually they told Dorothy that they no longer believed that she and Don had come to secretly eat the souls of their children!

About this time the Fairleys hired a cook and house helper named John Moubougou. This freed Ndoba to help Dorothy translate the Scriptures and to help Don. Dorothy also paid a local woman to wash the family's clothes at the river and watched them grow faded and threadbare from repeated poundings on rocks. With no clotheslines, the clothes were spread out on bushes to dry.

A certain species of fly occasionally visited their drying laundry to lay its eggs. When the Fairleys put on the infected clothing, their skin warmed the eggs, hatching them into tiny larvae. The larvae then burrowed into their skin, producing at first tiny boils that within a week grew to a half-inch in size. The boils were especially painful because the larvae periodically chewed on their hosts for nourishment. After about ten days, the larvae crawled out of the boils, usually at night. Once free, they wriggled away, leaving behind a significant crater. The larvae eventually developed into adult flies and flew off to find more clean laundry.

It was during this period that the Fairleys received a letter from Dr. Mason in Nyack, the director of all of the Alliance missionaries in Africa. He expressed his disappointment that in six months neither Harold Pierson nor Don Fairley had written to explain what exactly they were doing. So, at the end of one of his exhausting fourteen-hour days, Don sat down on a box in the smoky breezeway of the guest house. While the inevitable crowd of curious children cupped their hands over their mouths in amazement, Don typed by the light of his kerosene lantern a four-paged, single-spaced, apologetic reply to Dr. Mason: "We regret deeply your disappointment and embarrassment. We have been in the land now five months, and you no doubt will wonder what I have been doing during that time. . . . " For the remainder of the first term, Don faithfully wrote Dr. Mason a detailed report every two months!

At the end of September 1935, ten months after arriving back in the country, the Fairleys

finally moved into their new house. They had
no beds because the steel beds and basic furni-
ture that Don had ordered from the English
trader in January had been sold to someone
else before he knew they had arrived. So Don
made a wooden bedframe and tied the poles
together with vines. Dorothy sewed a canvas
cover over a homemade mattress of dried
grass, giving them a bed of sorts.

By this time the average attendance in the
morning and evening services averaged over
100, so Don built a large, open-sided meetinghouse that could seat a tightly packed crowd of
200. Don and Dorothy established a curricu-
lum of subjects that Mbadinga, Divingou and
Ndoba taught, including literacy classes, Bible
stories, simple doctrine, Scripture memoriza-
tion, personal and general evangelism, hygiene
and singing. During the evening meetings they
counseled the people on matters of witchcraft
and sorcery, ritual and vengeance poisonings,
ancestor worship using human skulls and the
practice of "soul slavery."

One day, soon after the main house was finished, a large group of Pygmies walked onto
the station. They brought gifts of dried antelope meat, a freshly killed gazelle and a baby
monkey for the Fairley children. They greeted
Don as their long-lost ancestor. The larger
workmen on the station were offended by the
Pygmies' boldness and made fun of them, ask-

ing if they thought that they too were men and not merely animals. To counter this attitude, Don and Dorothy went out of their way to show appreciation to and interest in the visitors, inviting them into their home and showing them how they lived.

The Pygmies were embarrassed by the missionaries' light skin, but were delighted at Dorothy and Bonnie Jeanne's long, straight hair. They were amused that Don and Dorothy and both their male and female child all ate together at the same table. In the meetings that day, Don pointed out that all races and sexes were created and loved equally by God and that Jesus died for all people, regardless of their size or appearance.

After everyone had eaten, Don and Dorothy invited the little people into their living room for a special service. Dorothy played her portable pump organ and, helped by their cook, Moubougou, the Fairleys sang. The Pygmies bobbed their heads and swayed to the music and, when the songs were over, rose as one person to examine the organ. It was apparently more than they could absorb in one sitting, so they filed out to the porch and talked in excited tones far into the night.

The following week Don had the workmen clear a nearby space on a hill overlooking the river and began work on a long, low bark house for the Pygmies. Once it was completed, they visited with increasing frequency, bringing meat and staying for a week or two of teaching before returning to their nomadic life in the forest.

Wild pigs also considered Bongolo their home. Traveling in herds of around 200, they ravaged plantations and left wide paths of destruction everywhere they went. They feared nothing except the leopard, but even the leopard thought twice before carrying off one of these succulent animals.

On one occasion, the villagers brought three little piglets to the Fairleys. The Fairley children were so enthralled by the animals that Don and Dorothy decided to keep them as pets. All three piglets initially grew well, but one of them was more vigorous than the others. Whenever they began to eat, this piglet would chew on their feet and ears until they squealed in pain. Don tried to separate the stronger one from the two weaker ones, but when he did, they pined and sulked until he gave up and put them back together. Eventually, the two weaker piglets died.

The surviving piglet was a female. The Fairley children named her "Snooty." She was given the run of the station and Dorothy even let the pushy little thing come into the house. During mealtimes Snooty would run from chair to chair, begging so appealingly that not even Don could refuse her. Once fed, Snooty squealed and grunted with such appreciation that they all had to laugh.

When she was about the size of a football, Snooty decided to befriend the Fairleys' pet chimpanzee, especially at feeding time. At first, the chimpanzee did not seem to mind sharing its food, but finally it grew weary of the game. Whenever Snooty got too greedy, the chimp would grab her by the tail or foot and swing her around until her little eyes bulged. Snooty seemed to enjoy this and squealed with pleasure. Even when the chimp slammed her back and forth on the ground like a ball on a string, Snooty would squeal like she was having the time of her life. When all else failed to dampen her friendship, the chimp climbed with her into a nearby tree, swung her around and around and finally let her fly. Snooty would sail through the air and hit the ground with a sickening thump, her round little body bouncing and rolling. Then she would squeal, jump to her feet and run off to find something else to do. It was like having a circus in the front yard.

Snooty loved to nose her way into the house and lie down at anyone's feet, begging to have her tummy scratched or her ears pulled. One day, Dorothy turned on the windup phonograph. Snooty jumped to her feet and began to sway in time with the music. As the music swelled, she rolled her eyes back in ecstasy, licked her lips again and again with her long, pink tongue and wiggled her tail from side to side.

Soon after discovering the phonograph,

Snooty heard the Fairley family sing. She was inside the house in a flash, performing her little dance and reducing the family to laughter. Several days later, as she was rooting around in the nearby forest, she heard the Christians singing in the church. She beat her way through the underbrush, ran through the church doors and found her way to the front. While the children choked back their giggles and Don and Dorothy struggled to keep their composure, Snooty danced with abandon. So as not to disrupt the service further, Don carried her out and put her in her pen.

Within a short time, Snooty learned to run to the church as soon as she heard the drums calling the people to come. When Don tried to keep her out, she would sneak in before he arrived and hide in a corner or under the benches until the music started. Time and time again, Don grabbed her and carried her out to her pen. She loved the music so much, however, that she would burrow under the fence until she escaped. Don finally had to bury the fencing a foot deep. When he realized that the people paid no attention to his dancing pig, he gave up. Snooty became a regular worshiper at the services.

Once the singing was over, she stretched out on her side and slept soundly through the entire sermon. When the music resumed, she was up in a flash and back in the front of the church next to the song leader, where she

swayed back and forth in pure delight in time
to the music, the clapping and the drums.

Snooty disdained dogs. Whenever a dog
came into the church, despite the hundreds of
people crowded together on log benches, she
sensed its presence and treated it like an evil
spirit. With the sureness of a bloodhound, she
would make a beeline for the intruder, advancing implacably under benches, legs and feet
until at last she had the enemy in sight and
drove him yelping from the church. If a man
picked up his dog and held it in his lap to protect it, she would jump on his legs until he released the dog and she could chase it out. The
dogs soon learned not to come to church.

Snooty also loathed dirt and mud and bathed
in the river every day, keeping herself as clean
as a baby. She was a pig, nevertheless, and did
not remain the size of a football. By the time
she was three years old, she was quite large.
The French government had opened an experi-
mental agricultural station in Lebamba in the
hopes of developing a new breed of pig. They
brought in European sows and boars and asked
Don if they could try to breed their boars with
Snooty. Don agreed. So Snooty was placed in a
pen in the agricultural station.

When she was in heat, a worker introduced
her to a handsome European boar. Snooty ut-
terly disdained him and crept around on her little cream feet with her nose in the air. She
would have nothing to do with the smelly thing

and the experiment ended in failure. Don finally took her back to Bongolo.

He eventually sent Snooty to another mission where she joined a shiftless herd of domestic pigs. Running with the wrong crowd, she fell into a life of crime, raiding village gardens big-time until she was captured and thrown in the pen. Her final end was . . . well, predictable and apparently quite delectable.

The Africans often brought to the station monkeys and chimpanzees whose mothers had been killed. Don made a practice of buying them, raising them to where they could fend for themselves and then setting them free on the station. One day someone brought him a baby gorilla.

When the little gorilla graduated from the bottle, Don taught him to sit at the table. He learned to eat, gazing at his white-skinned family with big brown wondering eyes. He watched carefully when he was shown something he was to do, and like a little man did just as he was told. He had a brown-haired cap over the top of his head and beautiful gray fur set off perfectly with patent leather black face and hands. Betty and Dottie loved to take him for walks. Like a perfect gentleman, he held their hands and walked with them wherever they went. When he was put to bed for the night he stayed there until he fell asleep.

The day came when amoebic dysentery rav-

aged the area and many people died. To the
Fairley children's great sorrow, the little gorilla
also fell ill and died a week later.

With Don's help, his children raised more
than seven chimpanzees. Because the animals
were so intelligent, the children were able to
teach them to wear clothes, sit up to the table
and eat with a spoon, drink water from a cup
and pour water for themselves. The last chimpanzee they raised from infancy was a female.
She not only learned to wear clothes, but also
learned to wash in a basin with soap, dry herself with a towel and powder her little black
and red face with a powder puff. Finally, she
learned to take a brush and brush her hair in
front of a mirror. At mealtimes, she sat at the
table, fed herself with a spoon and drank
through a straw. She also rode on the back of
the kids' bicycles with her arms around the
driver. The children had endless fun playing
with her. Most of the chimpanzees eventually
ended up in zoos in Germany, Switzerland and
England.

The large gardens that Don had so painstak-
ingly cleared and planted in September promised an abundant crop of manioc, taro,
peanuts, bananas and plantain, but before they
could harvest it, a herd of wild pigs came and
in one night destroyed nearly everything. Don
and his helpers replanted and built a fence
around the gardens, but the damage had been

done. It was six months before there was enough food for everyone.

So many people wanted to build a house and live on the mission property that Don was finally forced to limit the village to the sixty or so regular workers and their families who helped him burn and dig out stumps, keep clear the many paths and trails, build canoes, drag trees out of the river for safer navigation and construct more temporary houses.

The French administrator advised Don that he could not open an official school until there was a teacher with a diploma earned in France. But that did not keep Jean Mbadinga from opening a school for the boys that came with the workers and their wives. Boudiongo was the first chief to send his sons to the school and other chiefs in the area soon followed suit.

It was not just humans, however, that wanted Bongolo to be their home. For longer than anyone could remember, humans had avoided the site because of execution rock, abandoning it to the many wild animals in the area. Herds of wild pigs with viciously sharp, curved tusks regularly came through to forage, and large bands of several different kinds of monkeys lived high in the trees, shrieking and chattering at the invasion of humans below.

Twice a year herds of elephants crossed the river in the shallow water below the falls and foraged on both sides of the river. From time to time gorillas wandered into the gardens. The huge black apes were so heavy their feet left clear imprints on the hardened and polished paths. Even though they tore down ten to twenty banana trees at a time and ate the stalks, leaving the bananas untouched, Don would not allow anyone to shoot the gorillas.

It was the leopards, however, that nearly brought progress to a complete halt. A Frenchman had given the Fairleys a fox terrier. It was a faithful little watchdog, with short white hair and one black eye. Dorothy became especially attached to it. Ndoba suggested they call it Fougamou, the name of his home village. The name stuck.

One night as they were sleeping, Fougamou began to bark and to whine, running from door to door. Suspicious that there might be a wild animal prowling outside the house, Don got out of bed, turned up the low-burning kerosene lamp and took down his rifle. Dorothy held the lantern as he carefully opened the front door. They could see nothing beyond the circle of light, but Fougamou whined and cried so piteously that they closed the door and did not let the little dog out the rest of the night. In the morning they found in the dust under the eaves of the house the tracks of a large leopard. It had repeatedly circled the house during the night.

About a week later Don was paying the workmen near the chapel some fifty yards from the house with Fougamou at his side. Suddenly, a large leopard leaped out of the underbrush not more than twenty feet away. It happened so quickly that for an instant the men froze in astonishment and fear. The leopard pounced on the little dog, seized it in its mouth and disappeared into the forest. The men shouted and scattered in panic, but the leopard had what it wanted. When the pitiful yelping ceased, Fougamou was gone.

The leopards also fiercely contested the arrival of humans on the hills above Bongolo Falls. Hunting in packs of two or three, they carried off chickens and goats with disturbing frequency and at times even pawed at the walls of the bark houses on the station. When Don built a cage to protect the chickens from the leopards, a column of army ants came during the night and devoured them all.

The leopards were so numerous and so aggressive that they not infrequently preyed on the villagers themselves. The most terrifying series of attacks occurred near Mbigou. The claws of a very old leopard had cracked and frayed. Each claw, instead of being sharp, was frayed out at the end like a toothbrush, making it difficult for the animal to capture and hold onto the animals it seized. As a result, it began to stalk humans, a much easier prey.

The first clue that something was amiss came when a woman disappeared from her plantation, but since her body was never found no one could be certain what happened. A few days later, however, a second person disappeared in the same vicinity. The villagers searched the forest until they discovered the partially eaten body. In the weeks that followed, the leopard stalked and preyed on people who worked alone or in pairs in their plantations. One day it killed several men in a caravan. After this last attack, the leopard was seen to enter a dense part of the forest.

Ndoba explained to Don that the Eshira and Babongo peoples considered the leopard to be a sacred animal and the protector of their tribes. They considered themselves to be immune from the leopard and in no danger of ever being attacked. The secretary to the French administrator at Mbigou was an Eshira and, confident that he was of no interest to the leopard, offered to lead the hunters to its hiding place. The French Catholic priest from Mbigou had a shotgun and the Eshira talked him into coming along.

The men carefully searched the forest where the leopard had entered and eventually tracked it to a dense thicket of brush. Using Pygmy hunting nets and armed with spears, the men encircled the area and took positions around the net. The Eshira explained that he would flush the leopard out of the thicket toward the priest who would then have a clear shot. The man confidently disappeared into the thicket.

A moment later the waiting men heard a

blood-curdling scream followed by the leopard's roar and a great crashing in the brush as it fought and killed the Eshira. The men around the circle shouted to frighten the animal and the leopard turned and charged the net near the priest. The priest fired the gun at point-blank range. With the blood of his eleventh victim still dripping from its jaws, the leopard fell dead at his feet.

One evening as Don and one of his trusted men returned from checking on a work crew he spotted the spoor of an antelope not more than 100 yards from the main house. Concealed by brush and the roots of a tree, Don imitated the call of an antelope three or four times.

Just as he was about to call again, he heard Dorothy banging on a pot from the house, calling him to supper. He treasured the evening meal as the one time of the day when his family could be together without company. He handed the shotgun to his friend and, giving one more antelope call, slipped back onto the path home. He had not gone 100 yards when he heard the roar of the gun. Looking up to the darkening skies and smiling, he thanked the Lord for providing them once again with meat and continued on home.

About fifteen minutes later the Fairleys were well into their meal when they heard a group of men chanting as they did when they carried a large animal in from the forest. The noise was

much greater than the arrival of a mere antelope would warrant. The Fairleys stepped outside and were astounded to see an enormous
leopard lying dead on the ground. Don's antelope call had not attracted another antelope: It
had attracted a hungry leopard. It was the largest leopard any of them had ever seen. From
the tip of its nose to the end of its tail it mea-
sured nine feet.

Later, a group of leopards so terrorized the
people who lived on the station that they were
afraid to go to the gardens to work. Night after
night the workers lay awake listening to the
growling beasts as they prowled around their
houses, scratching the walls for openings. All
attempts to trap or shoot them proved fruitless.
Although the leopards usually hunted at night,
one day they came while everyone was away
from the main house. In broad daylight they
killed and devoured seven monkeys Don had
bought from villagers to free eventually. In des-
peration, the small band of missionaries and
Christians fasted and prayed that God would
intervene and send the leopards away. That
same week the leopards disappeared and never
returned.

9

War!

"They did not love their lives so much as to shrink from death." Revelation 12:11

By mid-October of 1936, Dorothy Fairley was eight months pregnant. Don was not prepared to deliver his third child himself, so he made plans for the family to travel to Mouila by caravan. He built a sedan chair for Dorothy, and for six-year-old Bonnie Jeanne and four-year-old Gordon he made two small chairs facing each other to be carried by four men. Others in the caravan carried the family's cots, bedding, mosquito nets, cooking gear, food and clothing.

By this time Don was used to walking long distances. Marching either at the head of the caravan or walking alongside the children, he had no difficulty keeping up with the toughened Africans. Knowing that Dorothy was uncomfortable, the men were touchingly gentle as they carried her over the rough trail.

Six days later, the caravan found the old Reo truck parked in the shade of a mango tree. Singing off-key as usual, the driver chauffeured them to Sindara as though it was up to him to bring on Dorothy's labor. After a steamy night on cots in the Hatton & Cookson warehouse, the family continued on to Lambaréné in a motorized launch. Three weeks later, Dorothy gave birth to Margaret Emma. Within a few days, the Piersons, including LeRoy, now free of tuberculosis, and George and Carol Klein, new missionary appointees, joined the Fairleys at Lambaréné and headed for Bongolo.

By this time, the French had built a road that reached to within twenty miles of Bongolo. The missionaries left the car and walked the rest of the way. When they finally arrived, they were greeted by an exuberant crowd of villagers who sang and danced in joyous welcome. Overwhelmed, the missionaries laughed and wept with the people. Bursting with pride at all they had accomplished, the Christians led the Americans up the steep hill along the cleared paths to the houses on the hill. Only Harold Pierson could appreciate the blood and sweat that had gone into what stood before them. He smiled and nodded to the beaming group to show his appreciation, but as usual said little.

The Kleins and Ozzie Pierson and LeRoy were shown through the two tiny, crude bark

and thatch houses Don had built in anticipation of their coming. It had taken them three
months and three days to travel from New
York City to Bongolo and during the entire
voyage they had somehow pictured things dif-
ferently. The harsh reality of living in two-room
bark huts with dirt floors, open fires and smelly
outhouses descended on them with jarring fi-
nality. Within days, Harold started construction on a permanent wooden house on top of
the highest hill on the station.

That year the Christmas story was read for
the first time in the Banzebi language. On
Christmas eve the Christians invited all the
people in the area to attend a great bonfire in
the center of the Bongolo clearing. Over 200
people crowded around the fire, singing and
listening to the story as it was told and retold.

Recognizing that burning one's fetishes was
an act of considerable courage, toward the
end of the program Don asked those who
wanted to follow Christ to stand, publicly
state their intentions and throw their fetishes
into the fire.

Burning a fetish did not necessarily mean
that a person had wholeheartedly put his or her
trust in Christ. It only meant that he or she
was taking a step of faith toward the light.
When, after destroying a powerful fetish, a person experienced no ill effects, he or she grew
more courageous and took several more steps

toward God. It frequently took two or three
fetish-burning occasions for someone to stop
trusting in them and destroy them all. That
evening twelve people stood and announced
that they had decided to follow Christ. They
then threw a large number of fetishes into the
fire.

Despite these initial demonstrations of faith,
on Christmas morning the missionaries felt
that only one person was ready for baptism—
Faustin Ndoba. The crowd stood or sat on
fallen trees or on the ground and watched as he
and Don waded fully clothed into the water
100 yards below Bongolo Falls. Don explained
that when he lowered Ndoba into the water it
would mean that Ndoba had chosen to die to
his old way of life and that when he lifted
Ndoba back out of the water it meant that
from that moment on Ndoba's life would belong only to God.

As Don lowered him into the water and lifted
him back out, the crowd watched in silence.
Ndoba wiped his face with his hand and signaled that he had something more to say. The
people strained to hear his voice over the noise
of the falls.

"Until now, my name has been Faustin
Ndoba," he said. "From this moment on, I
want to be called Paul. My name is no longer
Faustin, but Paul Ndoba!" Paul Ndoba and
Don Fairley dried themselves off with thread-
bare towels and the small band of Christians

pumped Paul's hand. Paul Ndoba was the first
man to be baptized in South Gabon.

With the arrival of additional missionaries, it
was now possible to divide up the work. By this
time eleven tribes were represented by the people living and attending the daily services on
the station. The Fairleys and Nzengue taught
the larger group of Banzebi, Bavoumbou, Mitsogo, Boumueli and Pygmies in the chapel.
The Piersons, Kleins, Jean Mbadinga, Paul
Ndoba and Marc Divingou taught the Massangou, Bapounou, Eshira, Bavarama and Ba-
voungou in a second temporary shelter. On
Sunday mornings everybody met together and
two interpreters translated.

Among the hundred or so who regularly attended the classes were thirty-seven men and
women, including eight couples whose faithful-
ness, zeal and newfound literacy prompted
their teachers to refer to them as "student
evangelists." From January through March the
missionaries spent extra time training this
group of thirty-seven in a short-term Bible
school. At Easter, the thirty-seven were baptized and, at the end of March, all eight couples and four single men scattered to their
respective villages to begin serving as evangelists. Among those baptized during the Easter
celebration in 1937 was Nzengue. At his baptism, he took the name Timothy.

There were two others of note in this group

of baptized believers: an intelligent and outspoken Mitsogo woman whose name nobody seems to remember and a young Massangou named Theophile Mouckagni who had grown up a slave in a Mitsogo village.

Some months before, a tall, serious-looking Bavoumbou named Etienne Lebongo had appeared on the station with his young wife. He ostensibly came to work, but it soon became apparent that he was deeply interested in the things of God. His language was distinct from any of the languages spoken at the station and although for weeks he sat silently through the church services never indicating how much he understood, he seemed to be listening intently to the teaching. The Bavoumbou were known as an aggressive and vigorous people steeped in witchcraft, ancestor worship and cannibalism. All the other tribes, including the Mitsogo, feared the Bavoumbou.

Although he was a stranger to the area, Etienne Lebongo understood the Yinzebi language reasonably well. One day, to everyone's surprise, he stood and confessed in broken Yinzebi that he was guilty of great sin against God and wanted to become a follower of Jesus. Could he be the key to ministry in yet another tribe?

The Fairleys were at last free to travel to the surrounding villages. Margaret Emma was less than six months old, so Don constructed a screened box for her that could be carried on a bamboo pole. Men carried the Fairley family, Dorothy's organ, food, pots and pans, bedding, a rifle and ammunition and gifts to present to the various chiefs.

At each village along the way, the caravan stopped. While Don greeted the chief and his elders, Dorothy and the "amazing" white children climbed out of their sedan chairs and Dorothy lifted Margaret out of her screened box. Everyone joined together to gawk at the strangers, touch their skin and smile when Dorothy greeted them in their language.

Once everyone had seen enough, Don presented the chief with a gift of soap or a machete and the chief in turn presented Don with a few eggs, a chicken or a goat for supper. Then, with the chief's permission, Don would have his men cut some poles and set up a tarpaulin for shade in the center of the village. When it was ready, Dorothy set up her organ and began to play. Soon a crowd would gather around the tarpaulin to watch and listen. Don and Timothy Nzengue would talk about God's plan for saving people from sin and death and invite them to follow Jesus. Nzengue would end the hour-long meeting by relating how he had decided to follow Christ and how his life had changed for the better. They visited an average of three villages a day, spending nights in the larger villages.

Etienne Lebongo was one of the porters on this trip, leading the caravan into the territory of his people, the Bavoumbou. When they reached his village, he went into his own house and without a word collected all of his fetishes. To his family's astonishment, he built a fire in front of his house and, standing next to the fire as if to guard it, burned them all.

Several days later the Fairleys met the chief of all the Bavoumbou people, a man named Mboudi. He listened attentively to the gospel message but did not at first believe. He did, however, ask Don to take his eleven-year-old son to learn at Jean Mbadinga's school in Bongolo. The boy's name was John.

This first trip also took them to Chief Kumiki's village. In the two years since Don had first visited Chief Kumiki, a Catholic priest had built a school and a chapel there. After exchanging greetings and news, Don reached into his bag and pulled out the chief's original walking stick. As the chief and his elders watched in curiosity, he carefully unwrapped it. The bright silver band at the top of the stick gleamed brightly in the sun. Chief Kumiki gaped in surprise. Then, with a shout of joy, he grabbed Don's hands and jumped up and down, laughing and shouting to his people until Don thought he was going to dance him across the village "square." It was a moment Don never forgot.

When he had calmed down, the chief held

the stick in his hand and studied the silver band, his fingers caressing the beloved carvings. His eyes caught the writing on the band.

"What does it say?" he asked in surprise. Don recited the verse to him in French, then recited it in the Yinzebi language. Chief Kumiki thought for a moment about the words, remembering that Don had talked about the Creator-God and His Son Jesus during his last visit.

"You have returned with my walking stick as you promised," he responded. "You have even made it better than it was. You are truly a man of your word." The old chief handed his substitute walking stick to Don.

"Please take this stick as my gift. You must come and teach my people. You must travel to all of our villages and teach our people about this Jesus. You have shown that you are a man we can trust." Don thanked the chief, but he and the old chief both knew that if he did what the chief asked, the Catholic priest would consider it a declaration of war. There was sadness in their parting.

Shortly after the Fairleys' trip, Harold Pierson made a similar trip to more than fifty Bapounou villages to the west and south. A group of nearly twenty young men returned with him to Bongolo. Within a two-month period most of them turned to Christ and burned their fetishes. Although they were still studying the language, the Kleins also made trips to the Massangou villages.

Every time Don or Harold traveled through Fougamou on their way to or from Port Gentil, Chief Kengélé asked them when they were going to send someone to teach his people. Ndoba was by now an effective preacher and evangelist. During his four years in Bongolo he had matured into a handsome young man. The missionaries had sent him out on numerous preaching missions and he had completed them despite danger and at times bitter opposition. He had also learned two languages and had proved himself to be a trustworthy, honest and faithful man of God. In October 1938, he and another missionary returned to Chief Kengélé's village to preach to the Eshira people.

The preaching and teaching of the first twenty student evangelists were enhanced by the increasingly frequent visits of the missionaries. Before several years had passed, hundreds of people throughout South Gabon abandoned the way of Mwiri and Bwiti to follow Christ and many more asked to know about the Jesus Way. The spiritual power evident in these new believers sent shock waves through the tribal societies. For the first time, it began to dawn on the previously unchallenged *ngangas* that the pitiful little band of Christians fanning out from Bongolo might present a serious challenge to their power.

The outspoken Mitsogo woman, who was baptized at Easter with the other student evan-

gelists, including Theophile Mouckagni, returned to the village of Ivouta and immediately
began to tell her people the Good News. Beginning with her immediate family, she taught
the Christian songs she had learned and read
the few Mitsogo Scriptures Marc Divingou had
helped translate. She eventually led her family
and some others to faith in Jesus Christ. She
told the new believers to have nothing more to
do with the ways of Bwiti and Mwiri and called
on the people of her village to worship the
Creator-God. She burned her own charms and
fetishes in front of her house and destroyed her
family idols. A small group of believers began
to gather in the very heart of Bwiti's power.

Theophile Mouckagni attended the meetings
in the widow's house but, fearing the Bwitists,
was careful to keep a low profile. He had married a girl named Pembe, the daughter of a
Bwitist.

Because the widow-evangelist would not respond to the threats of the village leaders, the
Bwitists and the ugly *nganga* of Ivouta decided
to kill her. Eventually they coerced someone in
the widow's household to slip poison into her
food. She became violently ill and after several
days died in agony.

The widow's death, however, ignited something deep inside Theophile. Within a week of
her burial, he threw caution to the wind and
took over the leadership of the group of disheartened believers in Ivouta. Previously, Theo-

phile had been timid, but following the widow-evangelist's death, he preached with an eloquence and a passion that astonished his hearers and stirred the hearts of many. Under pressure from her parents, his wife Pembe returned to them.

Theophile left Ivouta and traveled alone from village to village, preaching with greater and greater conviction. To the consternation and rage of the Bwitists and Mitsogo leaders, his preaching led ten times more people to turn away from the worship of Bwiti to follow the Jesus Way than the woman they had murdered. The *ngangas* made loud and angry threats to kill Theophile too, but he grew only stronger and bolder in his preaching. After much prayer on the part of the Christians and missionaries, Theophile's wife Pembe decided to defy her family and return to her husband's side.

Following the clear message of his martyred predecessor, Theophile called on the new Christians to publicly burn their fetishes and renounce both ancestor and spirit worship. In the village of Ivouta, the new Christians built blazing bonfires in the middle of the village and, to the horror of their neighbors, threw their sacred objects into the fire.

In response, Ivouta's most powerful *ngangas* drove poles into the ground directly in front of and around Theophile's house, covered them with fearful magic emblems and, chanting for all to hear, placed a terrifying curse upon Theo-

phile, his wife and all who followed Jesus.
When Theophile ignored the poles and
preached with even more power than before,
the same men who had poisoned Theophile's
predecessor gathered to plot his murder. Like
the giant fruit bats that swarm over a single
tree until its branches are black with their bodies, the Mitsogo *ngangas*, their helpers and ap-
prentices flocked to Ivouta to plan Theophile's
destruction and the annihilation of his band of
believers. Word spread through the village that
within days the *ngangas* would destroy the
Christians as effortlessly as they had destroyed
the widow-evangelist. Surely that would prove
that the white man's God was not available to
the African.

Tension began to mount in all of the Mitsogo
villages. The few Christians who were not too
frightened to associate with Theophile gathered around him and his anxious wife and
prayed for protection.

The long-awaited confrontation finally began
one night around midnight when a large group
of *ngangas* entered the village with flaming
torches, magic ebony sticks with heads carved
on them and a tightly woven box containing the
skull of a powerful Bwitist ancestor. The *ngangas*
placed these objects on the ground around the
little house where Theophile and Pembe lived.
As people in neighboring houses watched, the
ngangas buried other objects in the ground to
seal the Christians off from their source of

power. Others carried wood and built a huge bonfire directly in front of Theophile's house.

Far into the night they danced around the fire and around the house, chanting curses of death, sterility and madness upon the occupants. As the pounding of the drums increased, the *ngangas* whirled and leaped until the people watching in awe from cracked doorways no longer believed them to be merely human.

At the peak of the frenzy, the men lit pitch torches and, holding them high, danced around the house. Theophile, Pembe and about ten Christians inside the house alternately prayed and sang. The men outside moved closer and closer to the house with their torches, finally bringing them down to the thatch roof. But for some reason, and despite many attempts, the *ngangas* could not get the flames to touch the straw.

The *ngangas* abruptly broke from their dance around the house and returned to the fire to drink more *iboga* juice. Again they rushed at the house with their torches, but though they tried repeatedly they simply could not cause their torches to make contact with the tinder-dry palm roofing. As the hours passed, the torches and the bonfire burned lower and the dancing weakened. The first streaks of dawn lightened the sky and the drums and chanting wavered, then stopped. The exhausted priests of Bwiti, with their smoking torches, slunk into the forest to regroup.

When the *ngangas* had gone, Theophile and
his little band stepped out of the house into the
morning light and surveyed the scene. The people of the village also stepped out of their
houses to see what had happened. They
watched in amazement as Theophile and the
other Christians pulled up the sacred poles and
dug up the objects their tormentors had buried
in the ground. Piling everything on the embers,
the Christians unceremoniously reduced the
ngangas' precious objects to ashes.

That morning Theophile wrote a letter and
sent it by runner to Bongolo.

> Dear brothers in Jesus, our enemies have
> told the people that we are trusting in the
> white man to save us from them. They say
> that we have come to upset and to bring
> shame upon our leaders and upon our
> people and that we can only stand be-
> cause of the power of the white man.
> They accuse us of speaking publicly about
> sacred matters that should be kept secret
> and have denounced us to the people.
> Last night they tried to kill us, but God
> would not let them touch us. I have told
> them that God is living and present with
> us, that His Spirit is upon us and that we
> are not alone. We know that we are not
> alone, so do not come, do not approach
> us, but pray that here on this ground the
> people will know the truth that the Holy

Spirit of Jesus is present and that the Son
of God has power and authority.

The missionaries and Christians in Bongolo
were deeply disturbed by Theophile's letter,
but they recognized that he had cut to the
heart of the matter: Victory would only be total
if God demonstrated His power over Bwiti using African believers. That day and night the
Christians and missionaries at Bongolo fasted
and prayed for the tiny church of Ivouta.

The day was quiet and Theophile, Pembe
and the other Christians with them slept.
That evening the Christians again gathered in
Theophile and Pembe's house to pray and
sing. They knew that the *ngangas* would come
again.

Near midnight the priests of Bwiti returned
carrying torches and spears. Once again they
placed sacred objects and carved sticks around
the house and built a bonfire. Fortified with
iboga, they danced to the drums around the
bonfire. When they were ready, they each took
up a long, steel-tipped spear, encircled the
house and on a signal plunged their spears toward the flimsy walls. To their utter amazement, their spears never touched the bark
walls. Instead, they were deflected as though
an invisible shield stood between themselves
and the house. They tried repeatedly, but they
could not touch the house. Suddenly fearful,

they withdrew to the forest in confusion. When the sun came up the next morning, the *ngangas* had scattered like so many fruit bats.

The news of the Christians' victory at Ivouta rippled across the Mitsogo, Massangou and Banzebi villages in waves of hushed conversations. Theophile preached and traveled fearlessly and the Mitsogo church grew both in numbers and in maturity.

Although a major battle had been fought and won, the war was far from over. Every year the French government required each person to pay a head tax. Theophile and his wife paid their taxes with the small amount of support they received from the churches and from the Mission and received a receipt to prove they were paid.

One day several months after the confrontation with the Bwitists, soldiers from the government post came to Ivouta asking the people to show proof that they had paid their taxes. Theophile sent his wife to get their important papers. When he presented the receipt, the soldier in charge took it and tore it into shreds in front of them. It was their only proof of payment.

"This paper is from last year and is worthless!" the soldier said with a sneer on his face. "Where is your receipt from this year?" Theophile had just received the receipt and he and his wife knew the soldier was lying, but there was nothing they could do. As the people of

the village watched, the soldiers tied Theophile's and Pembe's hands behind them and
marched them out of the village to a work
camp several days away. The other laborers in
the camp had been arrested for failing to pay
their taxes and were forced to carry rocks for
the foundation of a government building
from the bottom of a riverbed up a steep
mountain.

At the time of her arrest, Pembe was seven
or eight months pregnant with her first child.
She was forced to work alongside her husband
from morning to night carrying rocks in a basket on her head up the mountain. The shelters
for the prisoners were open-sided, temporary
thatched roofs. During the cold nights Theophile and Pembe huddled together for warmth
on a woven grass mat covered only by a thin,
cotton cloth and exposed to the wind and
blowing rain.

In spite of their hardships, every morning and
evening the couple sang hymns, prayed together and told the other prisoners about Jesus
who had power to deliver those who followed
Him from both Mwiri and Bwiti. The soldier
who had arrested the couple singled them out
from the other prisoners and forced them to
eat their food uncooked. Although there was
water in the river below, he gave them dishwa-
ter to drink. Encouraged by his example, the
other soldiers also tormented Theophile and
Pembe, at one point beating them in an effort

to break their spirits so they would abandon the Jesus Way.

To the amazement of the soldiers, the more they mistreated them, the more God's joy seemed to pour from their hearts. The Spirit of God so possessed them and His power was so evident in them that after several weeks fear came upon all in the camp, prisoners and soldiers alike. Whispered news that the couple had been arrested under false charges through the influence of the Bwitists spread throughout the camp. The whisper turned to outspoken sympathy until finally the soldier who had arrested them came and set them free. Broken and humbled, he begged them not to tell the French administrator what he had done. Repaying the man's treachery with forgiveness, Pembe and Theophile kept silent and returned to Ivouta in victory and joy.

The gospel of Jesus Christ now took firm root among the Mitsogo people. The news of Theophile and Pembe's second triumph over the Bwitists rumbled through the Great Forest like an earthquake. Bwiti had been reduced to a second-rate power.

The Kleins left Bongolo for Lambaréné in December of 1937 for the birth of their first baby. On January 18, Carol Klein gave birth to twin girls at Schweitzer Hospital. Several days after the delivery Carol was up and about, but for some reason in the weeks that followed did not regain her strength as expected. The twins were small and, one month after birth, Alice, the smaller of the two, died.

As Carol cared for Lois Beth, the surviving twin, she experienced frequent dizzy spells. One morning, a week after Alice's death, she suddenly found it hard to breathe. A European doctor gave her an injection, but she continued to breathe with difficulty. The doctor noted that her pulse was fast and irregular. He diagnosed anemia.

One day, the nurses propped her up on pillows, but minutes later, her arms and legs stiffened and eventually her lower trunk and legs became paralyzed. Her hands also stiffened and turned inward. She was completely numb below the neck.

Several hours later, when George arrived, the doctor took him aside and explained that Carol could not possibly live for more than a few hours. Stunned, George entered the room and kissed his wife for what he feared was the last time. Kneeling by her bed, he and Carol cried out to God to spare her life. Almost immediately she sensed a warmth flow through her body. Her trunk and legs loosened up and, after an injection, her hands relaxed and returned to normal.

Dr. Schweitzer urged the family to return immediately to the United States for treatment. Unfortunately, the Kleins had left their papers and passports in Bongolo. George sent an urgent letter by boat and runner, explaining that Carol's life was in jeopardy. The news brought the missionaries and Christians at Bongolo to their knees. The Massangou Christians who had come to consider the Kleins as their own were especially disheartened. Harold Pierson asked Don to take a canoe and deliver the Kleins' papers to them as quickly as possible.

Early the next morning, Don and six oarsmen set out in the Mission canoe. The river was at flood stage and filled with trees and debris. Don took the rear paddle and directed the men to cut across every turn in the river to shorten the distance. Impelled by his urgency, the canoe seemed to fly downriver.

They were crossing the mouth of a tributary that entered the main river when suddenly a huge black object loomed out of the water in front of them. Don had only an instant to see the shape of a mother hippopotamus with her baby on her back. The men shouted in terror and leaned so far to the opposite side that for a heart-stopping moment water poured into the canoe. Don dug his oar into the water, sharply turning the boat. It missed the surprised behemoth by inches.

That evening in Mouila, Don hired a second canoe with eight fresh oarsmen who knew the river well. In a remarkable canoeing feat, the men rowed the entire night without slowing, arriving at Fougamou by daybreak.

It took Don all morning to find a ride over-

land to Sindara where he hired a third boat.
Ten powerful boatmen had arrived from the
east in a sleek twenty-foot canoe just the night
before. They agreed to take Don.

The rowers set off downriver at a speed
greater than anything Don had ever attained in
his launch. All night long the canoe surged forward without slowing or pausing, led by the
steady chanting of the man in front. Around
midnight a storm gathered ahead of them.
Flashes of light lit the sky, silhouetting black
clouds rearing high into the atmosphere. For
nearly an hour lightning streaked to the earth, il-
luminating the treacherous sandbanks and
sunken trees. Then, with a sudden gust, the
storm broke over their heads. There was a rush
of rain, then hail stinging their backs and arms
and rattling against the paddles. The hail lasted
only a few minutes and then more rain fell.
Through it all, Don felt a total absence of fear
and an awareness that the Lord was in the boat
with them as they sped on their mission of
mercy. In just forty-eight hours, he had traveled
350 miles by canoe. Don beached the canoe on
the shore below Dr. Schweitzer's hospital.

Barely able to walk, he was directed up the
hill to the house where the Kleins were staying.
George greeted him gratefully. The remaining
baby was barely alive and Carol was weak. Don
handed George his passports and important
papers and gave him the money he would need
for the trip home.

A tugboat was leaving that evening for Port Gentil. Don and George convinced the captain to take the Klein family on board. The men made a makeshift stretcher for Carol and set it on the forward deck. Little Lois Beth was placed in a screened box next to Carol's stretcher.

As night settled over them, the two men laid their hands on the mother and child and committed them to the care of Jesus. Long after the boat had disappeared into the dark, Don stood on the shore and prayed. Exhaustion finally overtaking him, he collapsed into bed at the Andendé mission. It would be eight years before the Kleins returned to Gabon.

Before returning to Bongolo, Don purchased a sack of cement and built a permanent marker for the grave of baby Alice Klein. It was the first American grave to be added to the cemetery in thirty years.

By 1938 the French colonial government had extended the dirt road, making it possible to drive from the coast of the French Congo to within about twenty miles of Bongolo. Friends from a church in the U.S. sent the Fairleys $700, so Don ordered a Renault pickup truck through one of the European traders in Mouila. Months later the riverboat chugged upriver with the vehicle on its lower deck. The battery was completely dead but with the help of twenty men they pushed it off the boat and started it.

Don traveled frequently to Mouila to pur-chase building supplies, beds, stoves, tools, hardware, fuel and food and to pick up the mail. At the end of each trip he parked the car at the end of the road and walked back to Bongolo. On one such trip a heavy rainstorm turned the road into a sea of mud. The car got stuck in the hills several kilometers from where the road ended. Don and the two African men who were with him decided to leave it there.

To avoid the mud, they walked along the top of a hill next to a thirty-foot, freshly cut bank. Unexpectedly, the edge of the bank gave way under Don's foot. He grabbed for a tree, but could not hold on. Falling headfirst down the bank, his head struck a half-buried rock and he was knocked unconscious.

Fearing they would be blamed, the two men with him fled, crossed the river and returned home without telling anyone what had hap-pened. Don lay unconscious on the bank for hours in the steady rain. When he regained consciousness, he tried to move, but even the smallest effort produced severe pain in his back. Nevertheless, he managed to roll onto his side and force himself to a sitting position. By now the sun was low in the sky. He called to the men who had been with him. When they did not answer, he realized they had fled.

Although the pain in his back was excruciat-ing, his arms and legs seemed to be all right. He slid down the bank to the road and tried to

crawl. That hurt too much. So he stood to his
feet and tried walking. The next several hours
were spent walking ten minutes, then resting
ten minutes. When he reached the river, he
waited and prayed until a man paddled by in a
canoe. The man took him across the river to
where the trail to Bongolo continued. As the
last light faded, Don staggered on for another
five kilometers before finally reaching the mission.

It was several months before Don could get
out of bed and walk without pain. X-rays taken
during the Fairley's subsequent furlough revealed that Don's fall had collapsed a vertebrae
in his lower back. He was now one inch
shorter.

By the summer of 1938 the Fairleys' daughter Bonnie Jeanne was nearly eight years old
and Gordon was six. There were no schools for
the children and, although Dorothy and Don
had taught the children to read, they had neither the time, materials or energy to school the
children further. The only other missionary
child on the station was LeRoy Pierson who,
although thirteen or fourteen years old, was
not receiving any formal schooling. He had
learned to both read and write the language of
the Bapounou people and spent much of his
time helping his mother translate hymns and
portions of the New Testament. He also
worked on the permanent house on the top of

the hill, helped supervise the workmen on the station and hunted game for food.

Dorothy spent her days from dawn to dusk preparing three meals a day over open fires, caring for her three children, gardening, canning meat and vegetables, receiving and entertaining the countless visitors that came to Bongolo, making sure that the clothes that her helpers pounded on rocks at the river to wash were respectably patched and countless other duties. In her spare time she kept the mission books, played the organ for meetings twice a day, translated hymns and Scripture portions, taught the women in short-term Bible classes, taught literacy classes and typed an average of one or two letters a week to supporters and family members back home. It was painfully clear that if the two oldest children stayed in Bongolo, they would remain unschooled.

Bonnie Jeanne was already two years behind her peers in the United States and both children had a poor command of the English language. What, Don and Dorothy asked themselves again and again before drifting off to sleep each night, would harm the children the most: separation for the next ten or eleven months or another year in Bongolo without schooling? Even a mother devoted to her children could see that without formal schooling, her children had a bleak future in America.

It was a choice no missionary today is required to face. With heavy hearts, Don and

Dorothy prepared their children as well as they knew for what lay ahead. On June 20, 1938, the entire family hiked out to the road and climbed into the Renault pickup to begin the 750-mile trip to Boma in the Belgian Congo. Except for the port city of Pointe Noire, during the entire five-day trip on dirt roads they did not pass a single car.

On June 30, a group of Alliance missionaries left the Belgian Congo for a year of furlough. Don and Dorothy entrusted Bonnie Jeanne and Gordon into the care of two of the single women. As the ship pulled away from the dock, its foghorn blasting, the children waved with excitement through the rusty railing, unaware of the deep sense of loss the parting would eventually bring. When the children could no longer see them, all pretense fell away. Holding onto each other and eighteen-month-old Margaret, Don and Dorothy wept.

The events of that year so taxed the Fairleys' emotional and physical resources that only by leaning more and more heavily upon God were they able to continue. As subsequent events would prove, it was not at all coincidental.

10

Power!

"His divine power has given us everything we need for life and godliness. . . ." 2 Peter 1:3

In April of 1939, the Fairleys left Bongolo on their second furlough, leaving the Piersons the sole missionaries of The Christian and Missionary Alliance in the country. Later that same year, Ray and Helen Cook arrived at the Bongolo mission.

Ray Cook proved to be an able and energetic administrator, builder and preacher. Despite thousands of man-hours of labor, the wooden house was far from finished. Marc Divingou had trained several carpenters to assist in the building and supervised the slow job of sawing the thousands of hardwood boards by hand and planing them smooth to a thickness of less than an inch.

Six months after the Cooks' arrival and in part thanks to Ray Cook's help, the house was finally finished. The day they finished the roof, Marc Divingou climbed down and announced that he no longer wanted to build houses. From then on, he said, he wanted to preach. Although he was the only fully trained carpenter, Harold Pierson agreed to let him go. In early 1940 the Cooks and Piersons moved into the new house.

On one of his furlough tours, Don met a wealthy Christian businessman named R.G. LeTourneau. LeTourneau was intrigued by Don's idea of building a hydroelectric plant at Bongolo Falls. In the months that followed their initial meeting, he instructed his engineers to help Don design a system for the Bongolo site. LeTourneau then purchased or manufactured everything that would be needed to build the plant.

During their last month in the U.S. before returning to Gabon, Don took welding lessons at LeTourneau's plant. He also recruited a burly Italian-American engineer named Furman Lentz to help him build the system. With additional gifts, he purchased a portable sawmill, a gasoline-powered generator, an electric welder, two brick presses and a Chevrolet Carryall station wagon. Excluding the car, the total weight of the materials and machinery came to nineteen tons.

Because of the instabilities of World War II and travel on the Atlantic, the Fairleys and other missionaries pondered and prayed about what to do with their children. In 1940 not a single school for missionary children existed in Central Africa. If their school-aged children were to have much of a future, the Fairleys decided, they would have to remain in boarding schools in the United States.

Bonnie Jeanne was nine and Gordon seven as the Fairleys' furlough drew to a close. The children begged their parents to take them back to Africa, but unless the Fairleys abandoned their mission and stayed in the homeland until their children were grown, they felt their only responsible choice was to leave them in the States. Don was convinced that God was leading them to return to Gabon without delay. Dorothy continued to struggle between duty to God and duty to her children.

In September of 1940 the Fairleys enrolled Bonnie Jeanne and Gordon in the Westervelt Home for Missionary Children in Batesburg, South Carolina. Thinking they would spare their children some of the pain of leaving, they slipped away from the school without saying goodbye. The unfortunate result was that this parting was the most painful the children would remember.

Arriving back at Bongolo, the Fairleys, Furman Lentz and Waldo and Cecil Schindler, new missionary recruits, were enthusiastically

welcomed by the Piersons, Cooks and a stead-
ily enlarging group of national believers living
on the station. The Fairleys moved back into
their old house which by now leaked badly.

Don and Furman immediately set about cutting a three-kilometer road linking Bongolo to
the new road the French had built through the
area. The materials and machinery were finally
delivered on a total of fifteen 300-mile trips
from the port of Pointe Noire in the French
Congo.

In 1941, shortly after the Piersons' arrival in
the United States for furlough, Harold developed pneumonia. Three days later his heart
failed. The medical authorities in attendance
wrote that his death at the age of fifty-one occurred from pneumonia caused by a massive
infestation of filaria.

While World War II raged in Europe, North
Africa and Asia, Furman Lentz, Don Fairley
and more than 100 African men, women and
teenaged boys built a hydroelectric plant next
to Bongolo Falls. The site they chose looked
impossibly rugged and overgrown for what
Don and Furman proposed to do entirely by
hand. Five- and six-foot high boulders stood
shoulder to shoulder, bound tightly to each
other and to the shoreline by vines and the
roots of enormous trees.

Initially all 100 workers attacked the site with
machetes and axes, eventually laying bare the

shoulder-high boulders above and alongside the falls. To further clear the work site they felled twenty to thirty large trees, cut them into moveable lengths and levered them out of the way. This allowed Don and Furman to trace out the foundations for the small building that would house the turbine, as well as the reservoir further upstream at the top of the falls. Retaining walls would divert water from the river into the reservoir.

Furman had the workmen build log fires over every large rock that stood in their way. After the fires had burned for twenty-four hours, the workers poured cold water over the heated boulders to split them. With strokes of his sledgehammer, Furman smashed the boulders into rocks small enough for the workmen to carry away. Within a few weeks they had removed by hand more than twenty tons of rock from the site.

Furman set up a motor-driven sawmill and cut the trees the workmen felled into boards to make concrete forms. During this time, Don made another trip to Pointe Noire to arrange for a Greek merchant to truck cement to Bongolo. Over the course of the project, the merchant trucked in a total of twenty-seven tons of cement.

That dry season, when the river dropped, the workmen poured a forty-foot long, ten-foot wide and twenty-foot deep reservoir out of steel-reinforced concrete and gravel. They also

built two-foot high walls out of stone and concrete to channel a portion of the river above
the falls into the reservoir. Simple wooden
gates controlled and regulated the flow of
water. Furman designed and built homemade
wooden cranes and, using block and tackle,
helped the workmen to load steel plates and
machinery weighing one and two tons onto
bamboo rafts or dugout canoes lashed together. They then paddled and poled the
loaded rafts and canoes across the river below
the falls to within thirty yards of the construction site. Had even one of the loads tipped into
the river, the project would have ended in failure. Astonishingly, not a single load was lost.

A five-foot wide "road" had to be cleared
ninety feet through a field of four-foot rocks in
order to bring the heavy machinery and equipment to the construction site. The women and
boys piled firewood on the rocks and kept fires
burning on them. Then, as with the earlier
boulders, they split the heated rocks by pouring cold water over them, until the path was
cleared. The men unloaded the steel and machinery from the canoes onto a wooden sled
with Furman's crane and, using block and
tackle, dragged the loaded sled up the "road"
the last ninety feet to the work site—much of it
done with enthusiasm and singing.

The most strenuous task involved bending
the heavy, eight-foot long, one-quarter-inch-
thick steel plates into cylinders with a sledge

hammer and a full-chain jack. Once the plates were bent, Furman and Don welded the sections together to form a steel tube four feet in diameter and seventy feet long that ran from the bottom of the reservoir above the falls into the turbine house at the foot of the falls. After welding the outside of the tube, they climbed inside and, in over 100-degree heat, welded it again from the inside. When the cylinder was tested, there was not a single leak.

The water turbine was welded into its housing and cemented into place at the end of the cylinder. A small house stood over the turbine. The shaft of the turbine rose into the floor of the house and was connected to a transmission which through a series of belts spun a generator to produce electricity.

Don had managed to purchase steel railroad ties to use as light poles. He had the workmen clear a path in the forest over 600 yards long running from the top of the cliff across the river from the light plant to all of the mission houses. At 100 foot intervals, he cemented his makeshift light poles into the ground and strung wires from the houses down to the river's edge.

When the construction was finished, Don began the complicated job of wiring the control boxes and generator. To his consternation, the instructions for wiring the generator were missing. Because of the war, it could take up to a year to obtain the necessary information through the mails. Unless he could figure out what to do, all of their work would amount to nothing. Worse, it would make the missionaries and their workers the laughingstock of the region.

Don had a small book on the principles of three-phase electricity, so during the next few nights he studied until he had it memorized. But the next morning when he looked at the wiring in the generator, he got confused. Locking himself into the little turbine house, he prayed for several hours, claiming for himself James 1:5: "If any of you lacks wisdom, he should ask God, who gives generously to all without finding fault, and it will be given to him."

After praying most of the morning, he attached the wires in a way that seemed to make sense and opened the water gates slightly. The powerful column of water flowed from the reservoir above the falls down through the tube to the turbine. Slowly, the turbine began to rotate, spinning the generator. Don sensed that the generator was laboring, so he shut everything down. He discovered that the fuses placed in the control panel at the factory were the wrong amperage and changed them. But when he tried again, the generator continued to protest. Somewhere there was a dead short in the system.

Rather than change the way he had connected the wires to the generator, Don checked the wires running from the electrical plant to the houses. There were three bare aluminum wires running in parallel and attached to glass insulators on the steel light poles. He followed the wires out of the turbine house and up onto the steel pole that stood next to the reservoir. Everything looked good. Joined by several of the Christian workmen who had waited and prayed outside while he prayed inside, he continued his inspection until he came to the last pole before the wires crossed the river to the Bongolo side. Something about the pole looked odd. And then he saw it, a mistake so glaring he could only laugh. The workman who had attached the lines to the pole the day before had correctly reasoned that the connection would be stronger if he bound the wires to the steel pole itself rather than to the glass insulators. He had carefully bound all three bare electrical lines to the steel pole, creating as dead an electrical short as can be made.

An hour later the mistake was corrected. This time, when the power was turned on, the entire unit operated smoothly and quietly with the precision of a great clock. To the amazement of the Africans who had never seen electric light, glass bulbs in all of the houses glowed brightly at the flip of a switch. Twenty-four-hour electricity had come to Bongolo!

Even as 100 workers built the hydroelectric plant, other workers hauled rocks from the river for the foundation of a second permanent house. When the foundation was complete, Don organized the men into competing teams on two brick machines, giving bonuses to the group that produced the most bricks in a day. Prior to the competition, the men were able to make only about 200 bricks a day. Once the competition heated up, the men made up to 2,000 bricks a day!

The first all-brick house took 80,000 bricks to complete. When it was finished and white-washed with the lime they had burned in the kilns, Ray and Helen Cook moved in, leaving the Schindlers in the wooden house on top of the hill and the Fairleys in the now-crumbling original mud and thatch house. As soon as the second permanent house was finished, Don began work on a brick house for his family.

The following year more and more Bavoum-bou turned to Christ and the Bavoumbou chiefs invited Don to come again to their villages to teach them. Missionary Waldo Schindler was still learning the Yinzebi language, but he accompanied Don on what was surely the most unforgettable trip of his life.

When they arrived at the edge of Bavoumbou territory, they were met by Etienne Lebongo, a large group of Bavoumbou warriors and Chief Mboudi, the territorial chief. Many of the men had painted their faces, parts of their backs, arms, legs and chests with the juice of the kola nut, giving them an almost otherworldly ap-

pearance. The chief and several of his officials
wore magnificent robes of woven raphia.

That night at Chief Mboudi's village Don
preached in Yinzebi and Etienne Lebongo
translated. At the close of the service Don
called on the people to turn from ancestor worship and sorcery to follow the living God. No
one was prepared for what followed.

Lebongo explained to the missionaries that
when families worshiped their ancestors, the
family members gathered in a corner or room in
the house where the ancestral objects were kept.
Forming a circle, they bowed and worshiped the
skulls and preserved body parts, chanting and
calling upon the departed spirits until they fell
into a kind of trance. Believing they were com-
muning with the spirits of their ancestors, they
would sing and sway in unison hour after hour.

Now, in response to Don's call to turn from
ancestor worship and follow the living God,
people collected their sacred objects—ancient
pottery, cooking pots, carved masks, polished
skulls of their ancestors, dried body parts—and
piled them in great heaps in the center of the
village. Then wood was stacked around them.
All the while, the people were singing a song
the evangelists had taught them:

> What can wash away my sin?
> Nothing but the blood of Jesus;
> What can make me whole again?
> Nothing but the blood of Jesus.

Shouting in jubilation, the people touched burning torches to the wood. As the flames licked at the wood, the village was enveloped with the stench and smoke of burning bones and dried flesh.

Preaching in other villages followed, but not all joined in the celebration. In every village there were those who refused to follow the way of Jesus, who stood and watched the proceedings in horror. One man fell at the feet of his uncle, begging him not to destroy the family's objects of worship and witchcraft. As the uncle carried the family's skulls, body parts and idols toward the bonfire, the other groveled at his feet and even licked and ate the dust in his path, imploring him and pleading with him not to expose the family to disaster. Weeping, he cried out that if the sacred objects were destroyed, their women would become sterile, their hunting nets and traps would bring no more food, death would sweep through their villages and they and their children would die. Shaking his feet free, the older man continued on resolutely until he reached the blazing fire. When he threw the armload into the flames, the other man screamed in anguish. The intensity and the emotion of such scenes at times so overwhelmed the missionaries that they wept.

As the missionaries traveled from village to village, the implication of what was happening rippled through the entire Bavoumbou society. In the evenings after the burnings, the new Christians built great bonfires and sat in a circle to sing and listen to each other tell how God had helped them turn to the light. This became a standard feature among all of the tribes. During these evening bonfire meetings, many who had remained undecided or who had not made a clean break with the past brought additional objects and burned them.

Usually the last objects to be given up were horns the *ngangas* had prepared for each person and which were supposed to contain their souls. Sealed inside these horns were hair, fingernails, toenails and secret potions. When a person traveled through enemy territory he went "body alone" and left his "soul house" hidden in his village or in a tree in the forest so that both the body and soul could not be destroyed. The people had such great faith in these objects that the Bavoumbou and Banzebi evangelists did not consider their people to be believers until they had destroyed these horns.

The trip through Bavoumbou country lasted nearly a month and took Fairley and Schindler to more than twenty villages. A great fear of the Creator-God fell on the people and a large portion of the population came to Christ in contrition and repentance. Chief Mboudi was among those who repented and turned to God. The power of Mwiri and Bwiti and the *ngangas* was swiftly eroding away.

In early 1942, Ray Cook and Paul Ndoba traveled north to Fougamou and preached to the Eshira people. Among those who decided to follow Christ was Ndoba's uncle Chief Kengélé, the chief of all the Eshira who in 1933 had entreated Don to establish the first Alliance mission station in his village.

That same year the Cooks left Bongolo with a large party of helpers including Paul Ndoba and Marc Divingou and their families and headed west and north into the Bapounou heartland. The new mission site was a level, heavily wooded area which they called Iléka. Within five years the missionaries and their helpers had established a strong Church numbering in the hundreds.

In 1944, Bert and Betty Corby arrived in Gabon and joined the Cooks at Iléka. The station eventually became as large and as important to the work in South Gabon as Bongolo, serving as a springboard to the planting of numerous other churches.

Jean Mbadinga remained in Bongolo several more years before moving to Iléka. During the ten years or so that he lived and worked in Bongolo, he taught hundreds of boys and young men to read and understand the Word of God. He also taught them a code of discipline, accountability and responsibility they had never known growing up in their villages.

Mbadinga's school was the first of its kind in the south, drawing together students from dif-

ferent, competing tribal groups. Mbadinga
helped them to accept each other as equals
and form lifelong bonds of friendship. In the
turbulent years that followed, these bonds of
friendship and respect would help prevent the
different groups from splitting along tribal
lines. Not surprisingly, many of his students
eventually became pastors and church leaders.

Jean Mbadinga was also one of the most
compelling role models the students would
ever know. Through his students, his impact on
the young Church reverberated for decades.
Because of his education and his fluency in
French, at the very outset of the work he was
able to accurately translate the Scriptures from
French, providing a key ingredient to the rapid
growth of the Bapounou Church. His impor-
tance to the establishment of the Church in
South Gabon cannot be overestimated.

11

Hunting with the Pygmies

"I have other sheep that are not of this sheep pen. I must bring them also." John 10:16

The first Pygmy chiefs to visit the Fairleys in Bongolo were Dépinga and Mbimba. Several months after their first visit they returned with the master hunter in that area of the country, a small man named Siombo. Siombo was always placed in charge of their hunting troupe because of his wide knowledge of the forest, the habits of the game and the locations of the trails. Don asked if he could accompany them on a hunt. Siombo agreed.

Don was ready to leave early that morning, but to his irritation the Pygmy hunters sat casually around their morning fire enjoying bananas. In answer to his impatient questions, they explained they could not leave until the sun had dried the rain on the leaves. Otherwise, their valuable bark hunting nets would be ruined.

About 10 a.m. they were finally ready. Don emerged from his house dressed in a khaki short-sleeved shirt, shorts, knee-high socks, sturdy shoes and his ever-present pith helmet. Over his shoulder, he carried his .410 gauge repeating shotgun. The Pygmy hunters reacted with consternation at the sight of the gun and insisted that he leave it behind. Don reluctantly returned the gun to the house and set out with them carrying a borrowed spear and a Pygmy net over his shoulder.

They soon joined up with the rest of the hunting party, which included men and women and the Pygmies' prized Basenji dogs. Basenji dogs cannot bark, but when excited they emit a strange kind of yelp that frightens the game. The dogs wore small wooden clappers stuffed with leaves tied to their necks to prevent them from rattling until the proper moment.

The group moved off silently onto an almost invisible trail through the tall trees and underbrush. About a mile into the forest the trail forked. A small clump of fresh leaves left by an advance scout was piled in the center of one of the trails. Siombo glanced at the leaves and took the opposite trail. Soon after, they encountered the scout who had located the animals. Without a word or even a sign, the group followed the scout, bending low under the tangled vegetation, at times crawling on hands and knees.

By this time, Don could discern on the rain-softened trail the hoofed prints of a variety of animals. Stopping next to a large tree downwind from a dense thicket of brush into which the hoofprints led, the leader initiated the setting of the nets. A scout was signaled around the far side of the thicket to see if the animals had finished feeding and had settled down to rest during the hottest part of the day. He soon returned, indicating with motions that there were no hoofprints on the far side of the thicket. The animals were resting deep inside the thicket.

Siombo wordlessly chose Don and half of the men to set up the nets and to be the "strikers of the meat." The rest he motioned to go to the far side of the thicket with the Basenji dogs to be the "bush beaters" and to await his signal that all was ready. As the bush beaters slipped away, carrying the excited but silent dogs in their arms, the strikers used sharp knives to clear the obstructing branches and leaves, tying the nets firmly to trees and bushes in a wide circle and pinning them to the ground with sharpened pegs pushed into the soft soil.

The men worked with remarkable speed and quietness, communicating with each other with birdcalls until all the nets were joined. When all but a twenty-foot section of the thicket where

the bush beaters would enter had been enclosed, the strikers, poised with clubs and
spears, spaced themselves at ten-foot intervals.
Don was placed between two tree trunks to
guard a short section of the net.

When all was ready, the beaters removed the
leaves from the dogs' clappers and, with a sudden shout, burst into the thicket. The noise
served to startle the prey into blind flight. A
horned and striped antelope shot from the
thicket like a missile, bursting through the net
and breaking free. Seconds later the screeching
dogs drove a second panicked antelope into
the nets. They held this time and the animal
was killed by an expertly thrown spear. The din
and the hunt within the enclosure continued
for another twenty minutes until it was clear
that no animals were left. When it was over,
the group gathered up several gazelles and an
antelope. The Pygmies bound leaves over the
animals' eyes, explaining that this prevented
the birds overhead from seeing that the animals were dead and spreading alarm to the rest
of the animals in the surrounding forest. The
same procedure was repeated several more
times that day.

Don's hunting trips and he and Dorothy's
persistent hospitality to the Pygmies resulted in
numerous invitations to visit Pygmy villages.
Although the Pygmies were nomadic, they did
build semipermanent villages where their

women planted gardens of bananas, plantain, manioc and other staple vegetables. They lived in these villages for several months of the year, then moved from camp to camp in the forest the rest of the year.

The Fairleys finally decided to visit several of the larger semipermanent Pygmy villages and organized a caravan to bring the entire family to Dépinga's village. After a trek of several days, the family arrived and were greeted by a four-foot chief named Nzamba. The Fairleys were shown to a lilliputian bark house in which they were to spend the night. Mrs. Fairley, pregnant and heavier than usual, could not get through the tiny door, so, while the women hid their amusement by cupping their hands over their mouths, the Pygmy men enlarged the entryway by removing a section of bark. Don also had the men remove the inside walls so they could put up their cots.

The little people crowded around the strangers, fascinated by their skin, clothes and movements. When the missionaries picked up forks and spoons and ate with them, the little people were astonished beyond words.

It was on this trip the Fairleys learned that for decades Pygmy women had been regularly taken as slave wives by the men of the big tribes, either by coercion, fear, witchcraft or outright capture. Once great bands, the Pygmy tribes had gradually declined to less than 3,000 people in the southern part of Gabon. Don estimated that in the fifty-mile area surrounding Bongolo there were less than 700, with only one woman for every four men.

Following their trip to the Pygmy villages, Don went to the French governor and appealed to him to outlaw the slave practice altogether. In response to Don's appeal, the governor decreed that all Pygmy slaves be freed. The decree stated that any slave owner who refused to free his slaves would be severely punished by the authorities. The local administrator went even further, giving Don full authority to intervene in any case of enslavement he found.

The Pygmies were overjoyed at this development and as Don traveled about he was frequently contacted and told where a Pygmy woman was being held against her will. Whenever this occurred, Don went immediately to that village and investigated. When asked, the women invariably chose to return to their people with their half-Pygmy, half-tribesman children. Within a decade the ratio of men to women nearly equalized in the Pygmy clans. As the mixed children intermarried with the Pygmies, the race grew larger and less distinct.

Men were sometimes taken in slavery as well. One of the slaves Don freed was Mbimba who was deeply scarred with smallpox. Some time later a group of Pygmies carried Mbimba to the Bongolo station with wounds caused by the horns and hoofs of a large antelope. Weak from pain and blood loss, Mbimba was laid on the floor of the Fairleys' house. Don and Dorothy prayed that God would spare his life. Dorothy closed his wounds with needle and thread and dressed them with bandages. To everyone's amazement, in a few days Mbimba was up. Taking Don's hands, he said, "Jesus is like honey in the mouth, satisfying the life within." Following Mbimba's decision to follow Jesus, several other men declared that they too had invited Jesus into their hearts. As time passed, more and more Pygmies followed Christ, abandoning fetishes they had purchased from *ngangas* and renouncing anger, hatred, unforgiveness and dishonesty.

At first only the Pygmy men stood in their frequent meetings on the station and talked openly about their new faith in Christ, but as more women were freed from their masters and returned to their villages, they too began to follow Jesus. The traditions allowed only men to speak in public gatherings, so the first time a woman stood to speak of her faith, the elders scolded her severely. Don gently intervened, explaining that although men's and women's roles and responsibilities were different, God loved them equally. Both should be free to praise God and give testimony in their gatherings. There followed many days of controversy, but finally the day came when complete silence reigned as these little sisters poured out their hearts. Within the space of seven years an entire clan of 122 Pygmies came to Christ.

Although the Lord helped the Fairleys to win the confidence of the Pygmies in the Bongolo area, other members of the Pygmy family in South Gabon remained untouched. When Don heard of a band 100 miles to the west of Bongolo in the forest near the new Iléka station, he determined to reach them with the message of Christ's love and forgiveness. It would prove to be more difficult—and exciting—than he imagined.

The Pygmy Christians from the Bongolo area suggested to Don that he take his heavy rifle with him, go into the forest and kill an elephant. Elephant meat was highly prized by the Pygmies and the Pygmy Christians were certain that if Don invited the distant clan to come and take some of the meat, they would respond with friendship. Besides, a short-term Bible school was soon to begin at the Iléka station and there would be plenty of meat left over to feed the students and their families.

John Moubougou, the cook, a Christian Pygmy hunter by the name of Nganza and a Bapounou who knew the forest well agreed to accompany Don for the hunt. Don had already obtained an elephant license from the French administrator.

Early one morning the four men climbed into the Chevrolet and headed west on the dirt road. When the road ended, they continued on foot. That evening they stopped in a Bapounou village to spend the night.

The next day Nganza and the guide set out into the mountains to scout for elephants while Don waited in the village. Several hours later the men returned with the news that they had sighted a herd tearing up a plantation. Assured that the hunt would not be long or difficult, Don took only a sandwich, a bottle of water, his Springfield .306 rifle and some ammunition.

By the time they got to the plantation, the elephants were gone, but broken trees and fresh spoor clearly marked their trail. They followed the herd's trail, moving farther and farther into the forest. Around noon Don realized that if they were to return to the base village by nightfall, they would have to turn around. "It's time to head back so we can make it to the village before nightfall," Don told Nganza.

"Back?!" the Pygmy exclaimed. "Couldn't we bow and ask the Great Chief of the skies and all the forest to give us an elephant? If we go back, we will never find an elephant!"

"We have to go back," Don insisted.

"The day is not over!" replied Nganza. "How can we abandon the hunt now? Let's go on!" Then he stopped and cocked his head. "Do you hear that?"

Don and his guide could hear the distant sound of an elephant crashing through the brush. "Elephants are not far off!"

The men jumped to their feet and headed toward the sound, taking care to remain downwind. They finally sighted a large male elephant that had been driven off from the main herd and was traveling alone. Despite their caution, the animal scented them and headed rapidly down a trail to a nearby river. He waded across the water, then disappeared into the forest on the far bank. The men followed but, after several exhausting river crossings, lost the trail and gave up.

By this time Don was determined to turn back, but a storm began to blow. There was nothing to do but seek shelter. The party, wet, cold and hungry, finally huddled in the roots of a huge tree.

The rain pounded relentlessly until darkness fell. Don had drunk all his water and, despite the rainwater he was able to catch and drink, he was thirsty beyond reason. Not a little irritated at their predicament, he turned to Nganza and asked, "Well, what do we do now?" He could barely see the little man's toothy smile in the dark.

"Oh," Nganza replied, "this is all right. We can spend the night here. No harm can come to us since the Good Spirit will take care of us. And you know," he added, "the Great Chief Jesus cares for us every day, both night and day. He never sleeps, so everything will be all right."

He must have seen the expression on Don's

face, because he added, "Why draw your forehead in wrinkles? We'll be fine." The guide said
nothing.

Late that night the rain stopped. The men
could hear the sounds of animals prowling in
the forest and crocodiles grubbing at the river
nearby. Don was alarmed. In the dark they had
little protection from prowling leopards. But he
kept his fear to himself.

Nganza suddenly turned to Don and announced that he was going to look for better
shelter for them. Ten minutes later he reap-
peared and led them to a deserted Pygmy
camp he had somehow located a quarter mile
away. Nganza showed Don into one of the
abandoned huts and busily stuffed fresh leaves
and sticks into the larger gaps in the dome of
the shelter.

"I'm going to go and bring fire," Nganza suddenly exclaimed.

"Where are you going to find fire?" Don
asked in astonishment. He had matches with
him, but the many river crossings had negated
the waterproofing. Nganza didn't explain, but
simply said, "I'm going." Apparently he had
smelled smoke from a distant Pygmy camp.

Don and his guide tried their best to sleep,
but the Pygmies' dogs had left thousands of
flea eggs in the village and, sensing human
presence, the eggs hatched, converged on the
little house and now swarmed over the aching
bodies of the frustrated hunters.

When Nganza returned, he was accompanied by a light-skinned Pygmy holding a blazing torch. He reported that earlier in the day he had encountered John Moubougou and a search party carrying food and a change of clothing. The search party was now at the Pygmy camp, one of dozens in this extensive section of virgin rain forest. The fire gradually died down and, as the smoke waned, hordes of mosquitoes filtered into the hut to add to the misery. It was the longest, most miserable night Don had ever endured.

At dawn, Nganza and the guide returned with John Moubougou. As though by magic, within half an hour he prepared hot coffee, freshly sliced pineapple and steaming pancakes with wild honey. Don ate the food gratefully. He would never again complain about a lumpy mattress!

When they had finished eating, Don asked Nganza if his Pygmy friend would take him to his village.

"No," he replied with a shake of his head. "Their attitude toward the white man has not changed. They do not want you to visit them. I told them all about the Jesus Way and I told them about you being a great hunter. I told them to come when they see you shoot an elephant." He must have sensed Don's dismay, because he added, "Today you're going to shoot an elephant!" There was little Don could do but go along.

They came to a wide river and saw from the torn up brush on the far bank that elephants had recently bathed on the shore. As they followed the trail of devastated trees and fresh spoor, Don's excitement rose. In the distance they could hear crackling and popping sounds as the elephants broke down small trees for food.

The trail led to the top of a nearby hill. Paying close attention to the wind, they approached cautiously to within 120 yards of the herd, hearing them long before they saw them. The hunters crawled forward on their hands and knees and, at last, Nganza pointed out a group of what appeared to be gray boulders 100 yards away. The elephants, standing perfectly still and sniffing the wind, sensed that something was wrong. Don stood up cautiously, the loaded gun to his shoulder. Out ahead of the herd stood a large male, his trunk lifted high as he drew in a great breath of air, his ears spread and his feet wide apart ready to attack. Don's knees were trembling with fatigue and excitement. Breathing a prayer for God to help him and apologizing in his heart to the beautiful animal, he sighted on the elephant's eye and squeezed the trigger.

An instant after the shot, the great male sank slowly to his knees, driving his tusks deep into the soft earth. As his body relaxed, his breath escaped from his lungs in a long, trumpeting bellow. At the sound of the shot, the rest of the herd stampeded upwind and into the forest.

Don forced his shaky legs to carry him to the side of the great animal. His bullet had entered just above the elephant's eye, killing it instantly. Over a ton of meat lay at his feet! Nganza whipped out his knife and cut off the elephant's tail. Waving it to heaven, he shouted, "Father God, thank You! You are the speaker of truth. You know all things. You are the giver of all great things!"

Carefully marking their trail as they went, the men left the carcass behind and headed back toward the Bapounou village. Within a short time, little people totally naked or wearing bunches of green grass or leaves as loincloths, appeared on the trail and led them to their camp. They were extremely shy when they saw Don, but as the light-skinned Pygmy explained to them that he had shot an elephant and that they were going to share in the bounty, they became more friendly, finally taking his hand in theirs and swaying back and forth in a sort of curtsy.

Don visited other Pygmy camps during the morning and at each camp Nganza recounted the entire adventure, including Don's night in the rain in a Pygmy hut without fire and how God had given them the elephant. When Nganza was finished, Don briefly told the little people the story of the Creator-God and His Son Jesus. It was so strange to their ears that they simply could not understand what he was talking about.

At the Bapounou village, they stopped and bathed in a nearby river, removing the imbedded ticks from their bodies, their clothes and each other. A runner had already gone to Iléka requesting the students and their wives to come with large baskets to help carry away some of the meat. They stripped the carcass of everything edible, including great quantities of fat. There was more than enough meat for everyone, including the Pygmies in the area and the people of the village in which Don had stayed. What could not be eaten within the next few days was smoked to be eaten later.

In the years that followed, missionaries and Pygmy Christians from the Bongolo clan visited and taught the Iléka clans. Many chose to follow Jesus.

12

Risking It All

"He will be the sure foundation for your times.
. . ." Isaiah 33:6

T here was a practical mission rule in the
Belgian Congo that was followed by missionaries in South Gabon until the 1950s. The
rule stated that since missionaries and their
children were always at risk of dying on their
remote stations from accidents, wild animals or
illness, each missionary family needed to obtain and store enough boards to make at least
one adult coffin. This was necessary because
boards were not widely available and took days
to cut by hand. The Fairleys kept their boards
in the attic of their house. On more than one
occasion, they came close to using them.

On November 30, 1941, Dorothy Fairley
gave birth at Schweitzer Hospital to her fourth

child, a girl they named Elizabeth Anne. Three years later she gave birth to their fifth and last child. Her name was Dorothy Louise. Despite her history of a weak heart, Mrs. Fairley weathered these pregnancies remarkably well.

But in 1944, two members of the Fairley family developed serious health problems. Eight-year-old Margaret contracted whooping cough, followed by measles. Then both she and Don fell ill with amoebic dysentery. By the fall, Margaret was so weak and pale that the Fairleys sent her with the furloughing Schindlers to join Bonnie Jeanne and Gordon in the States. Don was unable to find effective treatment in Gabon for his dysentery and by the time he and Dorothy left on furlough a year later, he weighed less than ninety pounds. It would take two years of recovery in the U.S. before they could return to Africa.

It was 1945. World War II was over and it was time for Don and Dorothy to take four-and-a-half-year-old Betty and fifteen-month-old Dottie home on furlough. After many disappointing cancellations on outbound converted U.S. military bombers, the Fairleys booked a flight on an aging French bush plane and headed up the west coast of Africa to Liberia where the chances of getting seats on a B-24 or B-25 transatlantic flight were much better. Military VIPs were accorded top priority, followed by rank and file military personnel, with civilians last. The Fairleys were so low on the list that they decided to move into a military barracks while they waited.

Finally, after two-and-a-half months, their turn came! A B-25 twin-engine bomber was ready. It would stop for refueling at the Azores, then go on to Brazil and finally to Florida. But on the eve of their departure, Don was notified that they were being "bumped" to make room for an American officer, his wife and very sick daughter who needed to get to the States for surgery. Though disappointed, the Fairleys were glad to help the girl.

A day or two following the departure, Don went to the post office to mail some letters. Inside he met a French friend.

"Why, Pastor Fairley," exclaimed the man, "I thought you were on the plane that left two days ago. How does it happen that you are here?" When Don told him that they had been bumped, the Frenchman responded, "I never expected to see you again. Word has just been received that the plane went down over the ocean with the loss of everyone on board!"

Convinced that their family needed to be together, in August of 1947 the Fairleys sailed from New York for Africa with all five of their children to begin their fourth term. Dorothy later wrote, "Those four years together in Africa were a most delightful and meaningful family experience. . . . The difficult separations [were] almost . . . forgotten as a result of those four happy years."

They arrived in Gabon to find a missionary force now totaling sixteen. George and Carol Klein had returned to Gabon, and Ray and Helen Cook, Waldo and Cecil Schindler, Bert and Betty Corby, Mary Ellen Gerber, Glenn and Ruth Harvey, Austin and Ruth Parliman, Floyd and Adah Shank and Enid Miller brought new energy and ideas to the work. Plans were underway to open new stations and, in Bongolo, Floyd Shank was constructing needed buildings and roads. The number of African evangelists and Christian workers now totaled eighty-four and the number of baptized believers in the south had grown to more than 450. Many young men and women were in training for the ministry and, at Bongolo, the first steel ferry was welded together.

When the Fairleys returned to the U.S. for their next furlough in 1951, Don was suffering from persistent hoarseness and a bleeding peptic ulcer. During the following year, he underwent surgery on his stomach and endured five operations on his vocal chords to remove inflammatory nodules. Health insurance for missionaries did not exist in those days and the Mission board had no funds to pay the costs of his medical care. Nevertheless, God provided the nearly penniless family everything they

needed to pay their bills before they returned
to Gabon for another four years.

It was the spring of 1953. Two days out of
New York, nine-year-old Dottie developed a
high fever. Suspecting malaria, Don treated her
with quinine and Dorothy wrapped her in a wet
sheet and kept a fan blowing on her to lower her
temperature. Despite their efforts, Dottie's condition worsened throughout the next day until,
by evening, she hovered near death.

The captain of the ship radioed a doctor in
New York for advice. After listening to the
symptoms, he advised the captain to take her
to Hamilton, Bermuda, the nearest port with a
hospital. That night, as Don held her in his
arms and prayed for his daughter's deliverance,
Dottie nearly died. When the ship docked, an
ambulance whisked her to the hospital.

The doctors insisted that her condition was
too critical for her to sail the next day. If the
entire family remained, the Mission would for-
feit their tickets on the freighter and would
have to purchase passage later at great additional cost. To save the Mission money, Don
and Dorothy made an agonizing decision: Don
would remain with Dottie until she recovered.
He would then come with her on the next
available ship. Dorothy and eleven-year-old
Betty would continue on to Gabon alone.

To comfort Dottie, Dorothy promised that
once she got to Africa she would order a "Toni"

doll for her, complete with several outfits and hair that could be combed and cared for just like hers. At the time they made the decision, Don and Dorothy did not know if Dottie would live or die or how they would pay for her care.

As Bermuda's shoreline gradually receded from sight, Dorothy wiped tears from her cheeks and reached for her Bible. A slip of paper fell to the floor. She read for the first time the words of a poem written by Esther L. Fields:

> Things don't just happen
> to us who love God,
> To us that have taken our stand.
> No matter the lot, the course,
> or the price,
> Things don't just happen,
> they're planned.

Greatly comforted, she returned the poem to her Bible. Two days later she received a radiogram from Don. Dottie had turned the corner and was recovering.

Don was given accommodation in a lovely home close to the hospital. One day, when Dottie was up and regaining her strength, the lady of the house took her shopping. "You can choose anything in the toy shop you want," the woman told her. Dottie spied a "Toni" doll and soon it was in the arms of its delighted new owner.

No diagnosis for Dottie's illness was ever found, but Don began to wonder how he would pay the hospital bill. God was already taking care of that. A large Presbyterian church in Hamilton was planning its 100th anniversary celebration. The pastor had invited prominent speakers from Great Britain, but, inasmuch as the church had been started by a missionary, he very much wanted a missionary to open the celebration. To his disappointment, no missionary was available. Several days later he learned that a missionary from Africa had arrived on the island with his sick daughter. The pastor invited Don to meet him at the church.

Don went, but still unable to talk because of the recent surgery on his vocal chords, he could only communicate by writing on a notepad. The pastor pulled a vial of oil out of his desk and anointed Don on the spot, asking God to heal him so he could preach the following week. The next Sunday, using a microphone, Don preached to the large congregation. His ministry was so appreciated that the church insisted on paying the entire hospital bill *and* Don and Dottie's tickets to fly to Africa.

As their ship pulled into port in Africa, Dorothy and Betty were surprised beyond words to see Dottie standing on the dock next to Don waving joyously and holding a beautiful new "Toni" doll!

One year later, Don was supervising the construction of a permanent church building at Bongolo when twelve-year-old Betty arrived from the Mission school some forty kilometers away. She had been sick with fever and abdominal pain for several days. Don had no formal medical training but, after examining her, he and Dorothy suspected appendicitis. They prepared a bed for her in the station wagon and headed for the government hospital eighty miles away at Mouila. Five hours later, the doctor confirmed their worst fears—she had appendicitis and would have to be flown to Pointe Noire.

A French surgeon operated on her that same evening. He found a perforated appendix and extensive peritonitis in her abdomen. When the operation was over, he sorrowfully told Don that Betty had one of the most serious infections he had ever seen. He had little hope she would survive.

For five days and nights Don nursed his feverish daughter. On the fifth day the doctor suggested that he "give her the last rites," as she would not last much longer. Don put his arms under his little girl and, lifting her up to God, thanked Him for giving her to them. He then invited God to take her home if that was His will. When he finished praying, God very clearly spoke to him the words of Psalm 118:17: "[She] will not die but live, and will proclaim what the LORD has done." Withdrawing his arms from under her, he whispered, "Betty dear, God has spoken to me and assured me that you will not die, but will live to honor Him." The words were no sooner spoken than Betty passed a large volume of gas. A short time later, color returned to her cheeks and new life flowed through her body. Later, the doctor took Don's hand and said simply, "It is a miracle. She has passed the crisis. She will live."

In September of 1954, a powerful storm blew a branch down on the power lines, breaking the top wire carrying current from the circuit breaker to the Bongolo houses. Don had two options: walk down the hill to the river, take the canoe across to the other side and shut the power off at the power plant or simply shut the power off to the broken wires using the circuit breaker behind his house.

It had been only one week since Don and Dorothy had returned from Pointe Noire with Betty, and Don was still weary. Against his better judgment, he decided to cut the power to the downed lines using the circuit breaker. There would still be power on the lines coming to the left side of the steel pole, but he would work on the right side.

After cutting the wire, he climbed twenty feet up a ladder until he reached the line that needed to be repaired. Taking care to stay well away from the "hot" left side of the pole, he tested the top wire on the right for current. There was none. He detached the end of the broken wire from the insulator and dropped it to the ground. Now he could find the two ends and splice them together. It was a simple matter and took only a few minutes to complete. All he needed now was several workmen to pull the wire tight between the poles while he reattached the end to its insulator.

Four feet from the end of the wire Don tied a rope and handed the end to the men on the ground below. He looped the rope up over the bracket holding the insulator. When the men pulled on the rope, the wire would be pulled up to the insulator and he could secure it. He had done it many times before.

The workmen tugged on the rope and, as it tightened, the end of the wire reached the insulator. Only one more foot of wire was needed to properly secure it. So, grasping the end of the wire with one hand, he urged the workmen to pull a little harder. After several unsuccessful tries, he climbed to the next rung of the ladder for better leverage. Once more he called for the workmen to pull on the rope. The men yanked the rope. The wire tightened for a second, then recoiled, throwing Don off balance. For a moment he hung in the air, clutching the unattached wire in one hand and falling slowly backward. Instinctively, he let go of the wire and with his right hand grabbed the steel pole. In the same instant, his left hand closed around the nearest object that could save him from falling—a bare wire attached to the left side of the pole.

Two hundred and twenty volts of electricity flashed through him, contracting every muscle in a relentless spasm he could neither control nor escape. For more than twenty long seconds he hung helplessly, unable to let go, unable to breathe, but fully conscious. With his head thrown back and his eyes rigidly open toward the sky, his mind told him that he could not possibly survive, that he was seconds from death. In that moment of agony, he saw a white cross in the sky above him. A thought flashed through his mind: *The way of the cross leads home!* Then, a second thought leaped insistently into his mind: *In order to live, I must let go.* As blackness closed in on him, with the last of his strength he pushed his feet off the ladder that still supported most of his weight. His body jerked toward the ground, its weight tearing his hand loose from the cable. He fell limp and unconscious onto the rocky ground twenty feet below.

At that same moment in Oregon, a friend of the Fairleys awakened from a sound sleep with an urgent and overpowering burden to pray for Don. Kneeling beside his bed, he cried out to God for Don's life. His wife was awakened by his loud praying and asked him what was wrong.

"I don't know," he replied, "except that I

seem to see Brother Fairley there in Africa up high and surrounded by flames!" He prayed for more than an hour until God lifted the burden from his heart.

The panic-stricken workmen ran to the house and yelled as loud as they could for Dorothy. She understood instantly what had happened and screamed for nurse Irene Ficke who had arrived in Bongolo only two days earlier. For the next two-and-a-half hours they administered artificial respiration until Don was finally able to breathe on his own. It was obvious to all that he had broken numerous bones, including some in his lower back. They decided not to move him until someone could drive the eighty miles to Mouila and return with the French doctor.

About thirty minutes after he began breathing on his own, Don finally regained consciousness. He was in terrible pain. Seeing feet all around him, he was briefly disappointed that he was still on earth. Then he heard Dorothy's voice encouraging him and silently thanked God for sparing his life. While twelve-year-old Betty stood crying on the porch, certain that her father was dying, Dorothy ran back and forth to the house bringing pillows and whatever else she could think of to make Don more comfortable. He lay on the ground for seven hours before the doctor arrived.

The doctor suggested that Don be carried into the house on some kind of stretcher.

Don himself suggested they use the black-board from a nearby schoolroom. Once inside the house, the doctor encased Don in a plaster cast that unfortunately never dried due to the high humidity and Don's abundant perspiration.

Several weeks later Irene and Dorothy removed the cast and Don cautiously began moving around in bed. He felt a grating sound in his lower back, and his right leg and right foot did not feel right. He also noticed that he was progressively losing vision in his left eye. Two months later, when Don was strong enough to travel, Dorothy drove him to Mouila, then flew to Lambaréné in a small French plane. When the plane made a stop en route, Don was so thirsty that he asked a waiter for a glass of water. Several hours later, they arrived at Schweitzer Hospital and Don was admitted.

Ten days after their arrival Don developed diarrhea, shaking chills and a continuously high fever. He had contracted typhoid fever, probably from drinking the contaminated water at the airport. It was ten days before the fever broke. Before Don had fully recovered, Dorothy developed a high fever from a kidney infection. By that time, Don had lost all vision in his left eye.

The doctors were finally able to x-ray Don's back and pelvis. They discovered that he had fractured his third and fifth lumbar vertebrae as

well as all of the ribs on the left side of his chest
close to the spine. The numbness in his right leg
and foot was due to compression of the sensory
nerves from the fractured vertebrae.

It was during this hospital stay that a friendship
developed between Don and Dr. Schweitzer. Dr.
Schweitzer admired Don for all that he had accomplished in the south in a relatively short period of time. And Don respected Dr.
Schweitzer for his devotion to his patients and
his concern about Don's welfare. But as the
weeks blended into months, Don felt more and
more burdened that for all his theological
knowledge Dr. Schweitzer did not know God.
The famous doctor was outspoken in his belief
that Jesus Christ was only a man, insisting that
Jesus Himself never claimed to be the Son of
God. He argued this point of view almost daily
in the hospital chapel services and consistently
and categorically refused to accept that Jesus
Christ was anything other than a good but mis-
understood man.

One day when Don was nearly fully recovered and able to take walks, he found himself
alone with Dr. Schweitzer. Taking a deep
breath, Don shared with him how he knew for
certain that Jesus Christ was the Son of God
and that He was very much alive. Dr.
Schweitzer stopped dead in his tracks. The
gentleness disappeared from his lined and
craggy face and his kindly features hardened.

"No!" he said grimly. "You are mistaken. I

will hear no more of it." He turned on his heels and stalked away.

Eight-and-a-half months after the accident, the Fairleys returned to the United States on an emergency medical furlough. Dr. Pischel, a prominent ophthalmologist in San Francisco, agreed to operate on Don's left eye even though the optimal time for surgery had long since passed and the eye was probably beyond repair. He was so intrigued by Don and Dorothy's confidence that God could perform a miracle through his hands that he decided not to charge for his services.

As the day of surgery approached, hundreds of people who knew the Fairleys prayed for a miracle. The operation went surprisingly well and Don's sight was completely restored. Although the Fairleys did not speak of their financial need to anyone but God, they once again received enough gifts to pay all of their hospital bills.

Three months after recovering the use of his left eye, Don no longer felt numbness in his leg and foot. He consulted an orthopedic surgeon to see if anything needed to be done about his back injuries. The surgeon examined him, reviewed his x-rays and finally called in another consultant. The specialists noted that although Don's back showed signs of damage, it caused him no pain and was functionally normal.

A month later, the Fairleys were back on the job in Gabon.

13

The History of the Acts of God in Gabon

"The kingdom of heaven is like a mustard seed.
. . ." Matthew 13:31

In September of 1956, Don and Dorothy Fairley returned to Gabon, the land to which God had called them twenty-three years before. By this time the missionary force they had spearheaded was led by George Klein and had grown to twenty-four missionaries working in five different locations throughout the south. In Bongolo, the new church building seated 1,000 people, a new dispensary had been opened and a new Bible school had been completed.

The number of self-supporting churches had

grown to seven; the number of baptized believers had climbed to over 1,000 and over 5,000 attended the weekly services. On June 29, 1956, the Gabon Alliance Church was formally organized with Marc Divingou as its first president, Paul Ndoba as treasurer and Jean Mbadinga as secretary.

In the beehive of activity that now characterized the work of the Mission and Church, the Fairleys' return barely created a ripple. They simply resumed their work where they had left off before Don's electrocution and fall. In subsequent years, the Fairleys left Bongolo to help establish churches far to the east. For his achievements in agriculture, community development and service, Don was decorated in public ceremonies by both the French colonial government and the post-independence government of Gabon. He never became field chairman. Rather, until his retirement from active missionary service in 1969, he served with quiet courage and humility under the leadership of younger men.

Dorothy Fairley died on July 29, 1982 in Mt. Angel, Oregon at the age of seventy-four. Don never recovered from the loss of his beloved wife and, until his death at the age of eighty-five, lived in anticipation of their eventual reunion in heaven. Today, in Gabon, the Fairley name is honored and revered by the thousands of believers whose lives were so profoundly changed by their coming.

In 1982, Dorothy Fairley dedicated her book, *In God's Plan, His Provision,* to her "five MKs, each born overseas: Bonnie Jeanne, Gordon Stuart, Margaret (Peggy), Betty Anne and Dorothy Louise, who shared in many of the experiences related here, all of whom are faithful followers of our Lord Jesus Christ." As of 1997,

Bonnie Jeanne and her husband Dr. Harold Draper, a cardiologist, are retired in Easton, Maryland. They have two daughters.

Gordon, an MAF pilot for fifteen years, and his wife Kathy June live in Keizer, Oregon. They have two daughters and one son.

Margaret (Peggy) married Richard Buck, an insurance claim specialist. They live in Meadow Vista, California and have two daughters, one son and seven grandchildren.

Betty and her husband, David Seng, a development engineer at Hughes Aircraft, live in Fullerton, California. They have two sons.

Dorothy (Dottie) is the wife of Alliance pastor, Rev. Roland Classen. They have three daughters and live in Snohomish, Washington.

From its tiny beginnings in Bongolo in 1935, the Gabon Alliance Church (called The Alliance Chrétienne du Gabon) in only twenty years spread into every province in the country. At the time of this writing (1997), its inclusive membership exceeds 45,000. The church is entirely self-supporting and self-governed. Enrollment at its two Bible schools stands at more than eighty and, with the help of its parent Mission, The Christian and Missionary Alliance, the Church is building a new campus for theological education in Libreville. It has a goal to establish churches among all of the remaining unreached people groups in the country within the next decade. It is Gabon's largest Protestant denomination.

Jean Mbadinga

In 1957, Jean Mbadinga was elected president of the Gabon Christian Alliance Church, replacing Marc Divingou. He served as church president until 1969. From 1985 to 1995 he was the senior pastor in a church in Moabi near where he was born. The Church he helped found has grown so rapidly in recent years that few of today's members are aware of his contribution.

Paul Ndoba

Paul Ndoba was elected president of the Gabon Christian Alliance Church in 1969 after John Mbadinga stepped down. He served as president until 1980 and until 1994 served as an assistant pastor at the church in Fougamou. He is loved and revered by the Church he helped establish.

Marc Divingou

After stepping down as church president in 1957, Marc Divingou preached among the Bapounou and served God faithfully until his death in about 1973.

John Mboudi

John Mboudi worked in the Bongolo dispensary until 1945 when he left to find work in Libreville in the French health service. In the early 1960s, he was chosen to go to France for training in Gabon's fledgling diplomatic corps and was subsequently sent to the Gabonese embassy in Washington, DC, where he worked as a consular official. In later years he served as Gabon's representative to the United Nations. Back in Gabon, he served in the presidential cabinet in various ministerial posts until his retirement.

Theophile Mouckagni

This fearless evangelist to the Mitsogo people served God with his wife in numerous Mitsogo and Massangou villages until the end of his life. He died of heart failure at the government hospital in Mouila in about 1975. A strong and vigorous Mitsogo church survives.

Timothy Nzengue

Timothy was the first convert from South Gabon to become an ordained pastor. He served as the pastor of the large Bongolo church until Sylvain Kivy Boudiongo was appointed in 1964. He died in 1994.

Chief Boudiongo

Despite fierce opposition from the area chiefs and his own people, Chief Boudiongo encouraged Pierson and Fairley to establish their mission at the Bongolo site. Some ten years later, he developed a strangulated hernia and died on Dr. Schweitzer's operating table. He was buried in Lambaréné.

Two of Boudiongo's sons eventually became pastors. The elder son briefly served as the pastor of the Bongolo church. The younger, Sylvain Kivy, also pastored at Bongolo and in 1975 planted the first church in Libreville which eventually grew to a congregation of 4,000 and produced eleven daughter churches.

The Pygmies

After the Fairleys retired from missionary service in Gabon, the Pygmies stopped coming in groups to visit Bongolo. The Bongolo area clan still considers itself to be largely Christian, but because no literate Pygmy Christian ever completed Bible school, the Church has no trained leaders and has drifted into error.

As of August 1997, a group of about sixty Pygmies is meeting with Alliance missionaries near the village of Oyem in northern Gabon. The Gabonese missionaries pledged $1,200 to help them build a chapel. The plan is meeting stiff resistance from the "big people" in the community.

Bongolo

The hydroelectric plant installed by Don Fairley and Furman Lentz on the Bongolo Falls produced electricity until 1992 when the government of Gabon built a dam and hydro-electric plant on the same site. The new plant now provides electricity for much of South Gabon.

In 1977, at the request of the Gabon Christian Alliance Church, a doctor and a team of five nurses joined the missionary force stationed in Bongolo. They established a nursing school, hospital, dental clinic, four outlying dispensaries and a primary health care team that serves a wide area. The Bongolo Evangelical Hospital has become the most important medical center for the southern third of Gabon. As of this writing, it has a staff of three missionary doctors, four missionary nurses and more than fifty Gabonese nurses, midwives, lab and x-ray technicians, administrators, chaplains, maintenance and yard men.

The Fairleys' house now serves as a dormitory for missionary children and all other original houses serve as homes for missionary teachers and medical personnel. Classrooms for the Bongolo Alliance School for Missionary Children now sit less than fifty yards from the first wooden house Harold Pierson and Don Fairley took four painstaking years to build. It is under the roof of that first permanent house that most of this book has been written.

On an average Sunday, approximately 750 people attend the two Alliance churches in the area.

In November of 1994, some sixty years after Don Fairley and Harold Pierson cleared the Bongolo site, the American, French, Canadian and Gabonese governments collaborated to build a 240-foot concrete and steel bridge across the Louétsi River. The bridge provides unrestricted access to the hospital and to the area's only secondary school, Paul Ndoba High School.

Every year thousands of patients come from all over Gabon to find healing at the Bongolo Evangelical Hospital. As they are treated, they hear the same story that a small band of Christians told their parents and grandparents in a tiny clearing in the Great Forest some sixty years ago. Hundreds each year still invite the Creator of the Great Forest and the Redeemer of its people to come and give them new life.

Epilogue

If History Ran Backward

W hat if history were to run backward to 1933 and God were to give our generation of Christians the same resources and ask us to do what these earlier missionaries did? Would we do it? Could we do it?

For the sake of the gospel would we agree to go to a place called "The White Man's Graveyard" without access to health care except by a four- or five-day canoe ride or overland trek?

Would we agree to keep a coffin in our attics to insure that others could bury us quickly if we or someone in our family died?

Would we agree to build our own house out of jungle materials and then live there for seven years as termites reduced it to rubble?

Would we cook over open fires and grow our own food?

Would we ungrudgingly work twelve-hour days and then spend the evenings translating the Scriptures and writing letters to our supporters and reports to our superiors? Or would we conclude that the task is impossible, the "door closed," the danger and privation too great, and sorrowfully turn away?

Would we take our children there?

Would we expose them to such terrible risks for the sake of people who may not even want us to come?

If there were a war and submarines were sinking the kinds of ships we had to sail on, would we board them with our families?

If war threatened to engulf the people we hoped to help, would we even consider leaving our families at home as do our country's military personnel and serve alone for long periods of time for the cause of Christ as did David Livingstone?

If our Mission organization did not cover the costs of our vaccinations or provide either health insurance or funds to help pay for the injuries and illnesses brought on by our service, would we resign in bitterness and just try not to think about the people we left behind?

If there were no Mission schools and few home-schooling organizations to help us, would we ever agree to deprive our children of the advantages of America for some hostile tribe on the other side of the earth?

If simple living took so much time and struggle that we did not have the time to give our children anything but a mediocre education, would we agree to a lifetime commitment to bring a nation to worship at the feet of Christ?

If history were to turn back to 1933 and we were asked to evangelize South Gabon with those same resources, would we not consider the job impossible?

I think that if it had been up to most of us, South Gabon would still be waiting. The comfort and security that our generation of Christians enjoys is lulling us to sleep. Nearly 2,000 years after the coming of Jesus Christ, whole nations remain completely unaware that the Creator-God came to earth to buy His people back with His own blood. "Therefore go," Jesus said, "and make disciples of all nations" (Matthew 28:19).

We are only the latest generation of Christians to wait and hope for the return of Jesus Christ, wondering why He is taking so long. The irony is that we hold the key to His return in our pockets and don't seem to know it!

Jesus was talking to His disciples about the end times when He made this statement: "And this gospel of the kingdom will be preached in the whole world as a testimony to all nations, and then the end will come" (Matthew 24:14). Jesus could not have made it clearer. The Messiah will return to earth when His Church does the job He gave it to do: Tell every people, nation and tribe in the world about Him.

Can we bring back the King? If peace, comfort and security mean more to us than anything else in the world, then God will just have to wait for a generation of Christians like the ones that brought the gospel to South Gabon.

But if we are willing to live by faith and obey God, we can do for all of the lost peoples of the world what the Fairleys did for the people hidden in the Great Forest of South Gabon.

Let us choose to be the generation that brings back the King.

Also by David Thompson

On Call

Book 3 in the
Jaffray Collection
of Missionary Portraits